Also by Keith Olbermann

The Worst Person in the World

The Big Show (with Dan Patrick)

TRUTH AND CONSEQUENCES

RANDOM HOUSE | NEW YORK

TRUTH AND CONSEQUENCES

*Special Comments on the
Bush Administration's War
on American Values*

Keith Olbermann

Published in the United States by Random House,
an imprint of The Random House Publishing Group,
a division of Random House, Inc., New York.

RANDOM HOUSE and colophon are registered
trademarks of Random House, Inc.

LIBRARY OF CONGRESS CATALOGING-IN-PUBLICATION DATA

Olbermann, Keith.
Truth and consequences: special comments on the Bush
administration's war on American values / Keith Olbermann.
p. cm.
ISBN 978-1-4000-6676-6
1. United States—Politics and government—2001– 2. United
States—Foreign relations—2001– 3. Bush, George W.
(George Walker), 1946– 4. United States—Social
conditions—1980– 5. Social values—United States.
6. Political corruption—United States. 7. Deception—
Political aspects—United States. I. Title.
E902.O43 2007
973.931—dc22   2007028254

Printed in the United States of America on acid-free paper

www.atrandom.com

9 8 7 6 5 4 3 2

Book design by Dana Leigh Blanchette

TO BOB ELLIOTT AND THE LATE RAY GOULDING,
who helped undo McCarthy with a weapon as
useful as Murrow's—humor—and who still
inspire and amaze

Contents

CONTENTS

Introduction

David Bloom was dead.

It was Sunday morning, April 6, 2003, and, as in the stuff of nightmares, somebody woke me up with the terrible news. He'd been on my old MSNBC show nearly every night in 1998, and in the week since we'd premiered *Countdown,* we'd spoken—via satellite—several times. And now he'd died from a blood clot in the middle of this new war.

I did what many of us do in times of crisis: I went to the ballpark. There was ineffable value in the chilly first weekend of the season at Shea Stadium in New York, where there would be at least a hint of spring and hope and the easing of mourning; where I could commiserate with news-savvy friends on the field like the Australian-born pitcher Graeme Lloyd, who'd wanted to know every detail I had about David's passing; where I could share the shock with friends in the press box; where I could dial back the pain through the simple ritual of folding up my scorecard and then filing out of the ballpark to the subway.

"Hey," one evidently drunken twentysomething fan said to his cohort just as I crossed through the press box hallway toward the exit ramp. "It's Keith Olbermann."

"Hey, Keith," his fellow staggerer began. Then a thought bounced across his brain like a shiny red ball skipping down the driveway toward traffic, and he stopped short. "Nah, forget him," he said to his pal. "He's a liberal."

I had been back at MSNBC for less than two months.

We had only launched *Countdown* six days earlier.

We had put virtually nothing on the newscast except reports from Iraq and Washington.

We had equally bashed Geraldo Rivera for giving away American troop positions on Fox, and Peter Arnett for giving an interview to Iraqi state television while also working on MSNBC.

We had sent David Bloom into harm's way and he wasn't coming back.

And I was not to be talked to because somehow I was a liberal.

BARACK OBAMA CALLED IT "9/11 fever" and we all had it, to some degree or another. The winter before, I'd actually kept a notebook with me in which to jot down the numbers of the subway cars I'd ridden in, just in case there was a biological attack. I could stagger into an emergency room one day and at least hand somebody a numerical trail of where I'd been. Maybe that could mitigate the impact of the terror. Even at the time I realized it was a psychological trick I was playing on myself to regain a false sense that I could control something in a world in which somebody had suddenly switched off the law of gravity. But as psychological tricks went, it was damned effective.

We played other tricks on ourselves in the eighteen months after the attacks. We, as the playwrights used to ask us to, suspended our disbelief.

As the naturally dubious, we reporters had severe doubts about the efficacy of blowing Iraq to hell. I even voiced them in my radio commentaries, couching them as gently as I possibly could. Others weren't so gentle and wound up losing their programs or getting death threats or having their wives' secret and truly patriotic careers exposed and ruined by those to whom patriotism is just a brand name.

Then the plotline in Iraq turned out to be not just phony, but also ridiculous. Not only were there no weapons of mass destruction, but the chemical warfare the generals and ex-generals nightly told us to expect also never materialized. Saddam Hussein not only had no offensive weapons, he didn't have many defensive ones. That summer, when it turned out our troops had staged a lightning raid to "save" Private Jessica Lynch from an Iraqi "military hospital" that didn't even have a Nurse Ratched in it, we broadcast the revised history as reported by a Canadian newspaper—the first TV news outlet in the country, I think, to do so. The right-wing water-carriers buffeted our management, and our management buffeted me.

But to that management's credit, the truth rapidly gathering behind the Hollywood story of "Saving Private Jessica" was sacrosanct to them.

They smelled the rats as surely as did I. Management only wanted to make sure I clarified that I wasn't attacking the heroism of the troops who broke into the hospital. *Of course I wasn't,* I thought to myself, *they were just as sincere as I had been.* Just as patriotic. Just as much—what was that other word beginning with "pat"?—oh, patsies.

That was the day my last symptoms of 9/11 fever disappeared.

The problem was that whatever kind of three-card monte game President Bush was running in Iraq, and whether he was the shill or just another victim, David Bloom was still dead, and so were a lot of young men and women in helmets whose names weren't David Bloom but who still counted every bit as much as he did.

THE WHITE HOUSE, of course, both fabricated and destroyed the rationale for the war, as well as the new American culture of fear first and ask questions later. It did the former through what has to be acknowledged as some very clever thinking, enabling the exploitation of 9/11 in endless ways: Watch the genuinely patriotic opposition voluntarily file in to the political equivalent of comedian Shelley Berman's famous "lousy hotel room"—the one he discovers seems to be missing all windows or doors or other ways out; cover Saddam Hussein in 9/11 guilt by association for the vast majority of people who couldn't tell al-Qaeda from Al Jarreau; grab all kinds of un-American powers over the American legal system the way President Adams tried to, or President Nixon, or Joe McCarthy, or anybody else who ever recognized inchoate fear in the public, who were as ever eager to protect their freedoms by surrendering them.

The problem for Messrs. Bush and Cheney and Rove, of course, was that having come up with a brilliant idea, they started to believe their own press clippings. Turns out they might not really have been that smart, or that good at execution.

Not a big deal, just the salvation of our democracy.

Just how bad this White House really was at the follow-through, I witnessed firsthand. At the height of the focused terrorism against Valerie Plame and Joe Wilson in the late spring and early summer of '04, we booked Joe to come on the show. Inexplicably, somebody in the administration's press office was working off an old script. They assumed I would be debunking Wilson, and decided to send me some helpful talking points by e-mail.

Only nobody there knew how to spell my name.

In the twenty-four hours prior to the interview, they must have sent a copy of the e-mail intended for me (Oberman, Olberman, Obermann, Obleman, Ohlbermen, Olderman, and Olberding, if I remember the permutations correctly) to seven different people at NBC whose names they could spell. These transmissions fell upon me like icicles on the first sunny day. Damned annoying. Damned stupid.

So of course, I showed the e-mail on *Countdown* and asked Joe Wilson about the talking points. And he laughed and I laughed and the audience ratings grew a little bit and I had an odd feeling that the show, and the country, would turn out all right after all.

WITH BITTER IRONY, it wasn't Iraq that did George Bush in—it was the weather.

Hurricane Katrina, provoking his governmental response of "Here's a bucket; that'll be a million dollars," ultimately was The Decider. Secretary of Homeland Security Michael Chertoff came on my television and declared "Louisiana is a city that is largely underwater," and I turned and shouted back at him, "There's your goddamned problem right there!" and switched on my computer and started spewing. We didn't call it that at the time, but that venting would become the first "Special Comment." And the attention it garnered dropped a few embers in the vast empty forests of my vast empty head, which would provide a lot of heat and a lot of light at the appropriate later date.

Oh, and parenthetically, prior to the attacks, had you ever heard the word "homeland" used in this country, except while somebody employed a cheesy German accent, and inwardly we were all glad anew that we'd beaten those bastards in 1945?

The Homeland?

Screw you, pally.

This is America.

ONCE AGAIN I'd learn a lot about this country on a baseball field.

I escaped to Florida at the start of March 2006, for my first trip to spring training in a decade. There are liberals and moderates and the enlightened and the skeptical within that sport, but they're outnumbered by the conservatives. Generally these are the conservatives of the more malleable sort. My best friend in the game is one of them. We've argued politics since 1990 and eventually he calls me a communist and I call him a fascist and then we start giggling and he begins to reminisce about hitting batters he didn't like with pitches.

And that day in '06 when I stepped onto the Yankees' practice field in Tampa, one of my other conservative baseball friends was waiting for me.

"What happened to my president?" he asked. "Was I not paying attention, or was he always like that?" I was stopped cold. He looked at me with angry eyes. "Katrina! What the hell did he do in New Orleans?" We had barely finished a conversation in which the political poles had so reversed themselves that I had partially defended Bush, when a second like-minded friend came over. "Am I nuts, or could you and I, just the two of us, have done a better job in the Gulf Coast than Bush and Chertoff and Mike 'Heck of a Job Brownie' Brown did? Just with paper towels."

I had a feeling the Democrats were going to do okay in the midterms.

THE ACTUAL PHENOMENON of the birth of the Special Comment has been recited so often by the barely contained egotist in me that I begin to feel like Ted Baxter explaining how it all started at a five-thousand-watt radio station in Fresno, California.

But the gist merits repetition (like you could stop me anyway). I was stuck on the tarmac at LAX, the late August thunderstorms in New York keeping us pinioned on the ground three thousand miles away with nothing to do but read the Associated Press stories on my ESPN-issued mobile phone.

And there it was: Don Rumsfeld calling me morally or intellectually confused, or the equivalent of a Nazi appeaser, or both. Not just me, mind you, but all of us—all of us who dared question Iraq, or the game of Simon Says that is the juvenile and ineffective new domestic counterterror rules, or the Bush administration itself.

And I searched the rest of that part of the Web offered me by the phone for the righteous indignation, for the atomic bombs of verbiage from the poets of the left, for the repudiation of this historically backward twisting of all that had happened since about 1933.

Nothing.

It was a moment, I gather, that some nonswimmers experience when a child falls into the deep water and nobody else makes a move. As time slowed, they invariably recall, they waited to see who else was going to dive in. Upon realizing nobody was, the thought formed, not of heroism or of urgency but of resignation. *Oh, hell, I see how this is going. I'm diving in. I wonder if I can swim.*

This does not always turn out well. Some drown, some don't, some prevail and everyone lives. But in the moment, you understand that if you're going to go down, at least you're going to go down for something worthwhile.

I started scribbling the first "Comment," by hand, on the back of my trip itinerary. We were somewhere over the Rockies by the time I finished.

THE RESPONSES to the pieces you will read herein were varied, but they contained one common thread.

I got fake anthrax mailed to my home, and the *New York Post* mocked me for calling the cops (when it turned out those cops would subsequently arrest a domestic terrorist who had done the same thing to David Letterman, Jon Stewart, and Sumner Redstone—kinda makes the *Post* pro-terrorist, right?). The FBI came and did a wonderful job, although it cost me a night in isolation at the hospital, and the clothes I was wearing, and, in an irony I recognized even at the time, that ESPN mobile device on which I had read Rumsfeld's remarks—burned in the irradiation of all I had on me when I opened the powder-filled letter.

They've threatened my relatives, printed phony stories about nonexistent skeletons in imaginary closets, guaranteed my imminent dismissal, and even whined when I started writing again for a memorabilia magazine about old baseball cards ("How can you let that lefty back in your page?" the editor quoted one complainant).

Baseball cards. Some people are dumb enough to see a political slant to frickin' baseball cards.

But amid all the tumult and the threatening and the name-calling, I have yet to see serious refutations of either the facts or the conclusions in these Comments.

Which leads me to the tentative conclusion that I'm probably right, with the caveat that I wish the water-carriers would apply to themselves as I apply it to myself:

As Oliver Cromwell said to the Church of Scotland nearly 360 years ago: *I beseech you, in the bowels of Christ, think it possible you may be mistaken.*

TRUTH AND CONSEQUENCES

1

Hurricane Katrina

September 5, 2005

While we didn't realize it at the time, and we hadn't yet enshrined the format or come up with the name, this was in fact the first Special Comment.[*]

I was on my way out to a minor league ballpark to clear my head of the first week of the cascade of disasters that was Hurricane Katrina, when I chanced to turn on the television. There was the secretary of Homeland Security—a John Waters look-alike without the charm— explaining to me that Louisiana was a city that was largely underwater. At first, the gaffe made me feel as if I were underwater. I needed to check that transcript to see if that's what he had really said.

Needless to say, I never made it to the ball game.

As I would later tell an interviewer, this was one of those moments when it felt like the words were just coming out of my fingers—when

---

[*]Just for the record: For the sake of utter (ahem) historical accuracy, these Special Comments have been reproduced in this book as I uttered them on the air, and that includes the sort of little grammatical infelicities that my copy editor tried to weed out. But what I said, I said, and I stand by it.

my indignation, more as a citizen than as a journalist, made it necessary to address a topic directly and at length.

And the words had not come out at that length in sixteen years. The only time I had ever previously written anything resembling, in shape, tone, or texture, the definition of the word "screed," I had been a local sportscaster in Los Angeles—angered and humiliated that when the 1989 World Series was interrupted by the Loma Prieta earthquake in the Bay Area, baseball staged no charity exhibition game, or promised any specific aid, even though the players wore on their chests the very names of the cities most heavily impacted by the disaster—San Francisco and Oakland. I pledged to donate the equivalent of the salary I would have made covering the series and challenged baseball's teams and players to do the same. The commentary lasted six minutes—six minutes out of a twenty-five-minute Sunday night sports broadcast.

When I got back to the office the next afternoon, the phones were still ringing, management was encouraging me to repeat the commentary on that evening's news, and the first reactionary newspaper columnist was comparing me (unfavorably, I should point out) to the character Howard Beale in the prescient movie *Network*. Almost all of the elements, good and bad, of the Special Comments were foreshadowed in those few days, principal among them that it was necessary to do and say things like this—but only when it *was* necessary, and not merely when it was rating "sweeps" time.

The next time it was necessary, for me anyway, was after Michael Chertoff faux-pas'd himself into the history books. For some, Hurricane Katrina was a lightbulb moment, when they realized that the president and administration in whom they had put their faith were in fact incompetent. For the rest of us, it was yet another case study in the dissonance between what they said and what they did. Like a lot of people, I was outraged as much by the administration's incompetence as I was by its apparent indifference to the people of New Orleans.

A day after I presented this Comment, Barbara Bush had her own Marie Antoinette moment, a jaw-dropping moment in which she was blissfully sanguine about the people huddled in the Astrodome: "And so many of the people in the arena here, you know, were underprivileged anyway, so this is working very well for them." Suddenly those murmurs, that "Bar" was not the benevolent grandmother implied by her carefully manicured image, had been confirmed. It was suddenly not hard to figure out either of the George Bushes.

The Katrina comment apparently struck a chord. It quickly made the rounds on the political blogs; my boss pulled me aside to encourage me to make similar remarks whenever the spirit moved me; *Rolling Stone* would put me alongside everybody from Jack Murtha to Seth MacFarlane in its year-end issue saluting "rebels"; and we even heard rumblings that the commentary was viewable in a pirated edition online, courtesy of some brand-new company called "YouTube"— whatever that was.

SECRETARY OF HOMELAND SECURITY Michael Chertoff said it all, starting his news briefing Saturday afternoon: "Louisiana is a city that is largely underwater . . ."

Well, there's your problem right there.

If ever a slip of the tongue defined a government's response to a crisis, this was it.

The seeming definition of our time and our leaders had been their insistence on slashing federal budgets for projects that might've saved New Orleans. The seeming characterization of our government: that it was on vacation when the city was lost, and could barely tear itself away from commemorating VJ Day and watching *Monty Python's Flying Circus* to at least pretend to get back to work. The seeming identification of these hapless bureaucrats: their pathetic use of the future tense in terms of relief they could've brought last Monday and Tuesday—like the president, whose statements have looked like they're being transmitted to us by some kind of four-day tape delay.

But no. The incompetence and the ludicrous prioritization will forever be symbolized by one gaffe by the head of what is ironically called "the Department of Homeland Security": "Louisiana is a city . . ."

Politician after politician—Republican and Democrat alike—has paraded before us, unwilling or unable to shut off the "I-Me" switch in their heads, condescendingly telling us about how moved they were or how devastated they were—congenitally incapable of telling the difference between the destruction of a city and the opening of a supermarket.

And as that sorry recital of self-absorption dragged on, I have resisted editorial comment. The focus needed to be on the efforts to save the stranded—even the Internet's meager powers were correctly devoted to telling the stories of the twin disasters, natural and government-made.

But now, at least, it is has stopped getting exponentially worse in Mississippi and Alabama and New Orleans and Louisiana (the state, not the city). And, having given our leaders what we know now is the week or so they need to get their act together, that period of editorial silence I mentioned should come to an end.

No one is suggesting that mayors or governors in the afflicted areas, nor the federal government, should be able to stop hurricanes. Lord knows, no one is suggesting that we should ever prioritize levee improvement for a below-sea-level city ahead of $454 million worth of trophy bridges for the politicians of Alaska.

But, nationally, these are leaders who won reelection last year largely by portraying their opponents as incapable of keeping the country safe. These are leaders who regularly pressure the news media in this country to report the reopening of a school or a power station in Iraq, and defy its citizens not to stand up and cheer. Yet they couldn't even keep one school or power station from being devastated by infrastructure collapse in New Orleans—even though the government had heard all the "chatter" from the scientists and city planners and hurricane centers and some group whose purposes the government couldn't quite discern—a group called the U.S. Army Corps of Engineers.

And most chillingly of all, this is the Law and Order and Terror government. It promised protection—or at least amelioration—against all threats, conventional, radiological, or biological.

It has just proved that it cannot save its citizens from a biological weapon called standing water.

Mr. Bush has now twice insisted that "we are not satisfied" with the response to the manifold tragedies along the Gulf Coast. I wonder which "we" he thinks he's speaking for on this point. Perhaps it's the administration, although we still don't know where some of them are. Anybody seen the vice president lately? The man whose message this time last year was "I'll Protect You, the Other Guy Will Let You Die"?

I don't know which "we" Mr. Bush meant.

For many of this country's citizens, the mantra has been—as we were taught in social studies it should always be—whether or not I voted for this president, he is still my president. I suspect anybody who had to give him that benefit of the doubt stopped doing so last week. I suspect a lot of his supporters, looking ahead to '08, are wondering how they can distance themselves from the two words which will define his government—our government: "New Orleans."

For him, it is a shame—in all senses of the word. A few changes of pronouns in there, and he might not have looked so much like a twenty-first-century Marie Antoinette. All that was needed was just a quick "I'm not satisfied with my government's response." Instead of hiding behind phrases like "No one could have foreseen," had he only remembered Winston Churchill's quote from the 1930s. "The responsibility" of government, Churchill told the British Parliament, "for the public safety is absolute and requires no mandate. It is, in fact, the prime object for which governments come into existence."

In forgetting that, the current administration did not merely damage itself—it damaged our confidence in our ability to rely on whoever is in the White House.

As we emphasized to you here all last week, the realities of the region are such that New Orleans is going to be largely uninhabitable for a lot longer than anybody is yet willing to recognize. Lord knows when the last body will be found, or the last artifact of the levee break dug up. Could be next March. Could be 2100. By then, in the muck and toxic mire of New Orleans, they may even find our government's credibility.

Somewhere in the city of Louisiana.

2

Feeling Morally or
Intellectually Confused?

August 30, 2006

As I've said, this was the first Special Comment, and I made it in response to then secretary of defense Donald Rumsfeld's speech at the American Legion's annual convention on August 29, 2006. Rumsfeld got a lot of flak for this speech—an op-ed piece in *The New York Times* by Frank Rich, statements from House Speaker Nancy Pelosi and Senate majority leader Harry Reid—and felt sufficiently under attack to respond to his critics in an op-ed piece of his own, in the *Los Angeles Times* a couple of days later. Herewith one unfortunate paragraph from that piece:

> *Then there is the case of Amnesty International, a long-respected human-rights organization, which called the detention facility at Guantanamo Bay the "gulag of our times"—a reference to the vast system of Soviet prisons and labor camps where innocent citizens were starved, tortured and murdered. The facility at Guantanamo Bay, by contrast, includes a volleyball court, basketball court, soc-*

cer field and library (the book most requested is "Harry Potter").
The food, served in accordance with Islamic diets, costs more per
detainee than the average U.S. military ration.

Let it not be said that we starve them or deprive them of volleyball. As for the waterboarding, well, we couldn't allow the *experience* to be nothing but a walk in the park . . .

Rumsfeld's original speech was a microcosm of the administration's approach to critics of the war: using specious historical analogies, countering straw-man arguments, and implying that said critics are unpatriotic or weak by using rhetorical techniques that allow them to deny they intended any such slurs. In this case, Rumsfeld suggests that critics of the war are the equivalent of people who wanted to appease the Nazis. The goal of these kinds of ad hominem attacks, of course, is to divert attention from the administration's fecklessness.

At the time I gave this Special Comment, I didn't yet know that the hypocrisy of this speech would turn out not to be limited to attacks on opponents of the war. Herewith, from the same address, another great moment in the Bush administration's big-lie, say-one-thing-and-do-the-opposite history:

The Department of Defense is proud to be your partner in the
Heroes to Hometowns program, which is helping severely wounded
veterans with job searches, with their homes, and with other activities to aid in their transition to civilian life.

As Dana Priest and Anne Hull would report five months later in *The Washington Post,* neither this "partnership" nor any other administration initiative came anywhere near the rat-infested confines of Walter Reed and other military hospitals, where badly wounded soldiers were making the transition from sacrifice to neglect. As the *Post* reported:

Disengaged clerks, unqualified platoon sergeants and overworked case managers fumble with simple needs: feeding soldiers' families who are close to poverty, replacing a uniform ripped off by medics in the desert sand or helping a brain-damaged soldier remember his next appointment.

While much of the discussion of the terrible and lasting effects of the administration's criminal lack of planning for life after the initial phase of the Iraq war justifiably focuses on its effects on the lives and futures of Iraqis, even after the exposés by *The Washington Post* and other media, there are, sadly, still books to be written on how this massive military mess and trauma will affect our soldiers, their families, and the communities to which they return.

THE MAN who sees absolutes where all other men see nuances and shades of meaning is either a prophet or a quack.

Donald H. Rumsfeld is not a prophet.

Mr. Rumsfeld's remarkable speech to the American Legion yesterday demands the deep analysis—and the sober contemplation—of every American. For it did not merely serve to impugn the morality or intelligence—indeed, the loyalty—of the majority of Americans, who oppose the transient occupants of the highest offices in the land. Worse still, it credits those same transient occupants—our employees—with a total omniscience, a total omniscience which neither common sense nor this administration's track record at home or abroad suggests they deserve.

Dissent and disagreement with government is the life's blood of human freedom; and not merely because it is the first roadblock against the kind of tyranny the men Mr. Rumsfeld likes to think of as "his" troops still fight, this very evening, in Iraq. It is also essential. Because just every once in a while it is right and the power to which it speaks is wrong.

In a small irony, however, Mr. Rumsfeld's speechwriter was adroit in invoking the memory of the appeasement of the Nazis. For in their time, there was another government faced with true peril—with a growing evil—powerful and remorseless. That government, like Mr. Rumsfeld's, had a monopoly on all the facts. It too had the "secret information." It alone had the true picture of the threat. It too dismissed and insulted its critics in terms like Mr. Rumsfeld's—questioning their intellect and their morality.

That government was England's, in the 1930s.

It *knew* Hitler posed no true threat to Europe, let alone England.

It *knew* Germany was not rearming, in violation of all treaties and accords.

It *knew* that the hard evidence it received, which contradicted its own policies, its own conclusions—its own omniscience—needed to be dismissed.

The English government of Neville Chamberlain already *knew* the truth.

Most relevant of all, it "knew" that its staunchest critics needed to be marginalized and isolated. In fact, it portrayed the foremost of them as a bloodthirsty warmonger who was, if not truly senile, at best morally or intellectually confused.

That critic's name was Winston Churchill.

Sadly, we have no Winston Churchills evident among us this evening. We have only Donald Rumsfelds, demonizing disagreement the way Neville Chamberlain demonized Winston Churchill.

History—and 163 million pounds of Luftwaffe bombs over England—have taught us that all Mr. Chamberlain had was his certainty—and his own confusion. A confusion that suggested that the office can not only make the man, but that the office can also make the facts.

Thus did Mr. Rumsfeld make an apt historical analogy.

Excepting the fact that he has the battery plugged in backwards. His government, absolute—and exclusive—in its knowledge, is not the modern version of the one which stood up to the Nazis. It is the modern version of the government of Neville Chamberlain.

But back to today's omniscient ones.

That about which Mr. Rumsfeld is confused is simply this: This is a democracy. Still. Though sometimes just barely. And, as such, all voices count—not just his.

Had he or his president perhaps proved any of their prior claims of omniscience—about Osama bin Laden's plans five years ago, about Saddam Hussein's weapons four years ago, about Hurricane Katrina's impact one year ago—we all might be able to swallow hard and accept their "omniscience" as a bearable, even useful, recipe of fact plus ego. But to date this government has proved little besides its own arrogance and its own hubris.

Mr. Rumsfeld is also personally confused, morally or intellectually, about his own standing in this matter. From Iraq to Katrina, to the entire "fog of fear" which continues to envelop this nation, he, Mr. Bush, Mr. Cheney, and their cronies have—inadvertently or intentionally—profited and benefited, both personally and politically.

And yet he can stand up in public and question the morality and the intellect of those of us who dare ask just for the receipt for the emperor's new clothes?

In what country was Mr. Rumsfeld raised? As a child, of whose heroism did he read? On what side of the battle for freedom did he dream one day to fight? With what country has he confused the United States of America?

The confusion we—as its citizens—must now address is stark and forbidding. But variations of it have faced our forefathers, when men like Nixon and McCarthy and Curtis LeMay have darkened our skies and obscured our flag. Note—with hope in your heart—that those earlier Americans always found their way to the light, and we can, too.

The confusion is about whether this secretary of defense, and this administration, are in fact now accomplishing what they claim the terrorists seek: the destruction of our freedoms, the very ones for which the same veterans Mr. Rumsfeld addressed yesterday in Salt Lake City so valiantly fought.

And about Mr. Rumsfeld's other main assertion, that this country faces a "new type of fascism":

As he was correct to remind us how a government that knew everything could get everything wrong, so too was he right when he said *that*—though probably not in the way he thought he meant it.

This country faces a new type of fascism indeed.

Although I presumptuously use his sign-off each night, in feeble tribute, I have utterly no claim to the words of the exemplary journalist Edward R. Murrow.

But never in the trial of a thousand years of writing could I come close to matching how he phrased a warning to an earlier generation of us, at a time when other politicians thought they and they alone knew everything and branded those who disagreed "confused" or "immoral."

Thus, forgive me for reading Murrow in full:

"We must not confuse dissent with disloyalty," he said in 1954.

We must remember always that accusation is not proof, and that conviction depends upon evidence and due process of law.

We will not walk in fear, one of another. We will not be driven by fear into an age of unreason, if we dig deep in our history and our doctrine, and remember that we are not descended from fearful men, not from men who feared to write, to speak, to associate, and to defend causes that were for the moment unpopular.

And so good night, and good luck.

3

"Have You No Sense
of Decency, Sir?"

September 5, 2006

President Bush gave a series of speeches on terrorism in the lead-up to the fifth anniversary of the September 11 attacks. The second of these speeches, his September 5 address to the Military Officers' Association, was part of a sustained effort to misdirect us away from the fiasco in Iraq and spare his party a bloodbath in the looming midterm elections. We know how that worked out. In addition to the usual mix of self-congratulation and fearmongering, the speech saw yet another tortured (pardon the pun) and offensive series of historical analogies.

IT IS OUR deep national shame—and ultimately it will be to the president's deep personal regret—that he has followed his secretary of defense down the path of trying to tie those loyal Americans who disagree with his policies—or even question their effectiveness or execution—to the Nazis of the past, and the al-Qaeda of the present.

Today, in the same subtle terms in which Mr. Bush and his colleagues muddied the clear line separating Iraq and 9/11—without ever actually saying so—the president quoted a purported Osama bin Laden letter that spoke of launching "a media campaign to create a wedge between the American people and their government."

Make no mistake here—the intent of that is to get us to confuse the psychotic scheming of an international terrorist with that familiar bogeyman of the right, the "media."

The president and the vice president and others have often attacked freedom of speech, and freedom of dissent, and freedom of the press.

Now, Mr. Bush has signaled that his unparalleled and unprincipled attack on reporting has a new and venomous side angle: the attempt to link, by the simple expediency of one word—"media"—the honest, patriotic, and indeed vital questions and questioning from American reporters, with the evil of al-Qaeda propaganda.

That linkage is more than just indefensible. It is un-American.

Mr. Bush and his colleagues have led us before to such waters.

We will not drink again.

And the president's rewriting and sanitizing of history, so it fits the expediencies of domestic politics, is just as false, and just as scurrilous: "In the 1920s a failed Austrian painter published a book in which he explained his intention to build an Aryan superstate in Germany and take revenge on Europe and eradicate the Jews. The world ignored Hitler's words, and paid a terrible price."

Whatever the true nature of al-Qaeda and other international terrorist threats, to ceaselessly compare them to the Nazi state of Germany serves only to embolden them.

Moreover, Mr. Bush, you are accomplishing in part what Osama bin Laden and others seek: a fearful American populace, easily manipulated, and willing to throw away any measure of restraint, any loyalty to our own ideals and freedoms, for the comforting illusion of safety.

It thus becomes necessary to remind the president that his administration's recent Nazi "kick" is an awful and cynical thing. And it becomes necessary to reach back into our history, for yet another quote, from yet another time, and to ask it of Mr. Bush:

"Have you no sense of decency, sir?"

4

This Hole in the Ground

September 11, 2006

I didn't know Mike Tanner was dead until September 24.

It was an awful bookending, but nothing approaching the kinds of things most New Yorkers, maybe most Americans, had found out in the days after 9/11. About Eamon McEneaney, I knew right away, that morning. He had been one of the heroes of the 1993 attack on the Trade Center; then, he had guided a "human chain" of survivors down a hundred flights of smoky stairwells. He worked on one of the uppermost floors. This time, there were no chains for him to lead, though no one who knew him has ever had a second's doubt that he tried.

Tanner was the starting quarterback, and McEneaney the starting wide receiver, in the first sporting event I ever covered for money. Fifteen dollars from United Press International to cover a Cornell football game in 1976—and wouldn't you know, the only thing that happened all day was Eamon dropping a punt that set up the other guy's field goal. Cornell loses 3–0 and I'm supposed to write 200 words about it, and telling the story as methodically as possible I only summon up about 110, and the UPI man in Albany says no, that's okay, I don't have to pad with 90 words on the early fall weather—they'll still send me the fifteen bucks.

I found out about Mike Tanner the way too many people found out about loved ones, or friends, or fellow alumni, or just anonymous (to them) smiling faces who suddenly counted every bit as much as those we knew.

His face and name were on a "Missing" poster on Canal Street.

I stopped and stared at it for five minutes. Missed a report I was supposed to file for KFWB Radio in Los Angeles. Somehow, the circumstances of finding out presaged, correctly, how much shock and pain there was yet to come.

I've said it, and written it, every time I've touched on, or been asked about, 9/11. Yes, I changed. Yes, I knew people. Eamon and Mike. And Tom Pecorelli from Fox Sports. And Ace Bailey from hockey. And even Barbara Olsen. Yes, I knew people in the building and on three of the four planes.

Yes, I started my career in the lobby of World Trade Center One. No, no relatives. No, I don't think my story is one of the first fifty thousand that should be told about that day.

But the point is, I have a story. And you do, too, probably. The lucky ones don't. Democrats have them and Republicans have them and those who thought the Iraq war made sense have them and those who knew it for what it was have them.

We are all in that sad thing together.

Unfortunately, as the fifth anniversary of 9/11 approached, Mr. Bush and the Republicans were making it clear that somehow their part of this enforced tragic togetherness was more important than their critics'.

The reaction to the first Special Comment had been like nothing I could have imagined. Views on YouTube and MSNBC.com and sundry other websites first doubled, then trebled, the number who had seen it on television.

If Secretary Rumsfeld wasn't replying directly to it in an op-ed piece he wrote two days later, his timing was to be commended. One of our guys called from the NBC bureau in Baghdad and said he'd read the script aloud to the staff in that hellhole and got loud cheers. My book shot from nineteen thousandth to sixth on Amazon. Harry Reid read some of it into the Senate record. My bosses asked me if I'd like to do them daily, or weekly, and I said I'd like to do them only as needed, that I would not and could not manufacture the requisite emotion. They dialed back quickly to encouraging me not to suppress that emotion.

And so, when I was told our *Countdown* on 9/11/06 would originate from a building right across from the still-empty hole in the ground where the Trade Center had stood, and would directly precede a speech in which the president would again try to make it seem as if he and the Republicans were the only true victims of the attacks, and the only true keepers of the flame, and the only ones capable of preventing another nightmare, I got to thinking of Mike Tanner, and I got mad.

HALF A LIFETIME AGO, I worked in this now-empty space. And for forty days after the attacks, I worked here again, trying to make sense of what happened, and was yet to happen, as a reporter.

All the time, I knew that the very air I breathed contained the remains of thousands of people, including four of my friends, two in the planes and—as I discovered from those "Missing" posters seared still into my soul—two more in the Towers.

And I knew, too, that this was the pyre for hundreds of New York policemen and firemen, of whom my family can claim half a dozen or more as our ancestors.

I belabor this to emphasize that for me this was, and is, and always shall be, personal.

And anyone who claims that I and others like me are "soft," or have "forgotten" the lessons of what happened here, is at best a grasping, opportunistic dilettante and at worst an idiot, whether he is a commentator, or a vice president, or a president.

However, of all the things those of us who were here five years ago could have forecast—of all the nightmares that unfolded before our eyes, and the others that unfolded only in our minds—none of us could have predicted this.

Five years later this space is still empty.

Five years later there is no memorial to the dead.

Five years later there is no building rising to show with proud defiance that we would not have our America wrung from us by cowards and criminals.

Five years later this country's wound is still open.

Five years later this country's mass grave is still unmarked.

Five years later this is still just a background for a photo op.

It is beyond shameful.

At the dedication of the Gettysburg memorial—barely four months after the last soldier staggered from another Pennsylvania field—Mr. Lincoln said, "We cannot dedicate, we cannot consecrate, we cannot hallow this ground. The brave men, living and dead, who struggled here, have consecrated it, far above our poor power to add or detract."

Lincoln used those words to immortalize their sacrifice.

Today our leaders could use those same words to rationalize their reprehensible inaction. "We cannot dedicate, we cannot consecrate, we cannot hallow this ground." So we won't.

Instead they bicker and buck-pass. They thwart private efforts, and jostle to claim credit for initiatives that go nowhere. They spend the money on irrelevant wars, and elaborate self-congratulations, and buying off columnists to write how good a job they're doing instead of doing any job at all.

Five years later, Mr. Bush, we are still fighting the terrorists on these streets. And look carefully, sir, on these sixteen empty acres. The terrorists are clearly still winning.

And, in a crime against every victim here and every patriotic sentiment you mouthed but did not enact, you have done nothing about it.

And there is something worse still than this vast gaping hole in this city and in the fabric of our nation. There is its symbolism of the promise unfulfilled, the urgent oath reduced to lazy execution.

The only positive on 9/11 and the days and weeks that so slowly and painfully followed it was the unanimous humanity, here and throughout the country. The government, the president in particular, was given every possible measure of support.

Those who did not belong to his party—tabled that.

Those who doubted the mechanics of his election—ignored that.

Those who wondered of his qualifications—forgot that.

History teaches us that nearly unanimous support of a government cannot be taken away from that government by its critics. It can only be squandered by those who use it not to heal a nation's wounds, but to take political advantage.

Terrorists did not come and steal our newly regained sense of being American first and political fiftieth. Nor did the Democrats. Nor did the media. Nor did the people.

The president—and those around him—did that.

They promised bipartisanship, and then showed that to them, "bipartisanship" meant that their party would rule and the rest would have to follow, or be branded, with ever-escalating hysteria, as morally or intellectually confused, as appeasers, as those who, in the vice president's words yesterday, "validate the strategy of the terrorists."

They promised protection, and then showed that to them "protection" meant going to war against a despot whose hand they had once shaken, a despot who, we now learn from our own Senate Intelligence Committee, hated al-Qaeda as much as we did.

The polite phrase for how so many of us were duped into supporting a war, on the false premise that it had "something to do" with 9/11, is "lying by implication."

The impolite phrase is "impeachable offense."

Not once in now five years has this president ever offered to assume responsibility for the failures that led to this empty space, and to this, the current, curdled version of our beloved country.

Still, there is a last snapping flame from a final candle of respect and fairness: Even his most virulent critics have never suggested he alone bears the full brunt of the blame for 9/11.

Half the time, in fact, this president has been so gently treated that he has seemed not even to be the man most responsible for anything in his own administration.

Yet what is happening this very night?

A miniseries created, influenced—possibly financed—by the most radical and cold of domestic political Machiavellis continues to be televised into our homes.

The documented truths of the last fifteen years are replaced by bald-faced lies; the talking points of the current regime parroted; the whole sorry story blurred by spin to make the party out of office seem vacillating and impotent and the party in office seem like the only option.

How dare you, Mr. President, after taking cynical advantage of the unanimity and love and transmuting it into fraudulent war and needless death, after monstrously transforming it into fear and suspicion and turning that fear into the campaign slogan of three elections—how dare you—or those around you—ever "spin" 9/11?

Just as the terrorists have succeeded—are still succeeding—as long as there is no memorial and no construction here at Ground Zero, so, too, have they succeeded, and are still succeeding, as long as this government uses 9/11 as a wedge to pit Americans against Americans.

This is an odd point to cite a television program, especially one from March of 1960. But as Disney's continuing sellout of the truth (and this country) suggests, even television programs can be powerful things.

And long ago, a series called *The Twilight Zone* broadcast a riveting episode entitled "The Monsters Are Due on Maple Street."

In brief: A meteor sparks rumors of an invasion by extraterrestrials disguised as humans. The electricity goes out. A neighbor pleads for calm. Suddenly his car—and only his car—starts. Someone suggests he must be the alien. Then another man's lights go on. As charges and suspicion and panic overtake the street, guns are inevitably produced. An "alien" is shot—but he turns out to be just another neighbor, returning from going for help. The camera pulls back to a nearby hill, where two extraterrestrials are seen manipulating a small device that can jam electricity. The veteran tells his novice that there's no need to actually attack, that you just turn off a few of the human machines and then "they pick the most dangerous enemy they can find, and it's themselves."

And then, in perhaps his finest piece of writing, Rod Serling sums it up with words of remarkable prescience, given where we find ourselves tonight:

> The tools of conquest do not necessarily come with bombs and explosions and fallout. There are weapons that are simply thoughts, attitudes, prejudices, to be found only in the minds of men.
>
> For the record, prejudices can kill and suspicion can destroy, and a thoughtless, frightened search for a scapegoat has a fallout all its own—for the children, and the children yet unborn.

When those who dissent are told time and time again—as we will be, if not tonight by the president, then tomorrow by his portable public chorus—that he is preserving our freedom, but that if we use any of it, we are somehow un-American; when we are scolded that if we merely question, we have "forgotten the lessons of 9/11" . . . Look into this empty space behind me and the bipartisanship upon which this administration also did not build, and tell me:

Who has left this hole in the ground?

We have not forgotten, Mr. President.

You have.

May this country forgive you.

5

Bush Owes Us an Apology

September 18, 2006

I gave this Special Comment in response to President Bush's angry and combative news conference on September 15, 2006. The gathering capped a week of heavy presidential lobbying over the shape of terror-detainee legislation under consideration by the Congress. The day before, a defiant Republican-led Senate Armed Services Committee had voted in favor of legislation that extended more legal protections to suspects than the president wanted. When questioned about a letter sent by former secretary of state Colin Powell to Senator John McCain reminding him of the dire consequences of the administration's detainee policies, the president had responded with anger and an alarming statement of the administration's increasingly limited view of our right to challenge our leaders.

THE PRESIDENT of the United States owes this country an apology.

It will not be offered, of course. He does not realize its necessity.

There are now none around him who would tell him or could.

The last of them, it appears, was the very man whose letter provoked the president into the conduct for which the apology is essential.

An apology is this president's only hope of regaining the slightest measure of confidence of what has been, for nearly two years, a clear majority of his people.

Not "confidence" in his policies, nor in his designs, nor even in something as narrowly focused as which vision of torture shall prevail—his, or that of the man who has sent him into apoplexy, Colin Powell.

In a larger sense, the president needs to regain our confidence that he has some basic understanding of what this country represents—of what it must maintain if we are to defeat not only terrorists, but if we are also to defeat what is ever more increasingly apparent as an attempt to redefine the way we live here and what we mean when we say the word "freedom."

Because it is evident now that, if not its architect, this president intends to be the contractor for this narrowing of the definition of freedom.

The president revealed this last Friday, as he fairly spat through his teeth words of unrestrained fury directed at the man who was once the very symbol of his administration, who was once an ambassador from this administration to its critics, as he had once been an ambassador from the military to its critics.

The former secretary of state, Mr. Powell, had written, simply and candidly and without anger, that "the world is beginning to doubt the moral basis of our fight against terrorism."

This president's response included not merely what is apparently the presidential equivalent of threatening to hold one's breath, but within, it contained one particularly chilling phrase.

"Mr. President, former secretary of state Colin Powell says the world is beginning to doubt the moral basis of our fight against terrorism," he was asked by a reporter. "If a former chairman of the Joint Chiefs of Staff and former secretary of state feels this way, don't you think that Americans and the rest of the world are beginning to wonder whether you're following a flawed strategy?"

"If there's any comparison between the compassion and decency of the American people and the terrorist tactics of extremists, it's flawed logic," Bush said. "It's just—I simply can't accept that. It's unacceptable to think that there's any kind of comparison between the behavior of the United States of America and the action of Islamic extremists who kill innocent women and children to achieve an objective."

Of course it's acceptable to think that there's "any kind of comparison."

And in this particular debate, it is not only acceptable, it is obviously necessary, even if Mr. Powell never made the comparison in his letter.

Some will think that our actions at Abu Ghraib, or in Guantánamo, or in secret prisons in Eastern Europe, are all too comparable to the actions of the extremists.

Some will think that there is no similarity, or, if there is one, it is to the slightest and most unavoidable of degrees.

What all of us will agree on is that we have the right—we have the duty—to think about the comparison.

And, most importantly, that the other guy, whose opinion about this we cannot fathom, has exactly the same right as we do: to think—and say—what his mind and his heart and his conscience tell him is right.

All of us agree about that.

Except, it seems, this president.

With increasing rage, he and his administration have begun to tell us we are not permitted to disagree with them, that we cannot be right, that Colin Powell cannot be right.

And then there was that one most awful phrase.

In four simple words last Friday, the president brought into sharp focus what has been only vaguely clear these past five and a half years, the way the terrain at night is perceptible only during an angry flash of lightning, and then, a second later, all again is dark.

"It's unacceptable to think," he said.

It is never unacceptable to think.

And when a president says thinking is unacceptable, even on one topic, even in the heat of the moment, even in the turning of a phrase extracted from its context, he takes us toward a new and fearful path—one heretofore the realm of science fiction authors and apocalyptic visionaries.

That flash of lightning freezes at the distant horizon, and we can just make out a world in which authority can actually suggest it has become unacceptable to think.

Thus the lightning flash reveals not merely a president we have already seen, the one who believes he has a monopoly on current truth.

It now shows us a president who has decided that of all our commanders in chief, ever, he alone has had the knowledge necessary to alter and reshape our inalienable rights.

This is a frightening, and a dangerous, delusion, Mr. President.

If Mr. Powell's letter—cautionary, concerned, predominantly supportive—can induce from you such wrath and such intolerance, what would you say were this statement to be shouted to you by a reporter, or written to you by a colleague?

"Governments are instituted among men, deriving their just powers from the consent of the governed. That whenever any form of government becomes destructive of these ends, it is the right of the people to alter or to abolish it, and to institute new government."

Those incendiary thoughts came, of course, from a prior holder of your job, Mr. Bush.

They were the words of Thomas Jefferson.

He put them in the Declaration of Independence.

Mr. Bush, what would you say to something that antithetical to the status quo just now? Would you call it "unacceptable" for Jefferson to think such things, or to write them?

Between your confidence in your infallibility, sir, and your demonizing of dissent, and now these rages better suited to a thwarted three-year-old, you have left the unnerving sense of a White House coming unglued—a chilling suspicion that perhaps we have not seen the peak of the anger, that we can no longer forecast what next will be said to, or about, anyone who disagrees.

Or what will next be done to them.

On this newscast last Friday night, constitutional law professor Jonathan Turley of George Washington University suggested that at some point in the near future some of the "detainees" transferred from secret CIA cells to Guantánamo will finally get to tell the Red Cross that they have indeed been tortured.

Thus the debate over the Geneva Conventions might not be about further interrogations of detainees, but about those already conducted, and the possible liability of the administration for them.

That certainly could explain Mr. Bush's fury.

That, at this point, is speculative.

But at least it provides an alternative possibility as to why the president's words were at such variance from the entire history of this country.

For there needs to be some other explanation, Mr. Bush, than that you truly believe we should live in a United States of America in which a thought is unacceptable.

There needs to be a delegation of responsible leaders—Republicans or otherwise—who can sit you down, as Barry Goldwater and Hugh Scott once sat Richard Nixon down, and explain the reality of the situation you have created.

There needs to be an apology from the president of the United States.

And more than one.

But, Mr. Bush, the others—for warnings unheeded five years ago, for war unjustified four years ago, for battle unprepared three years ago—they are not weighted with the urgency and necessity of this one.

We must know that, to you, thought with which you disagree—and even voice with which you disagree, and even action with which you disagree—are still sacrosanct to you.

The philosopher Voltaire once insisted to another author, "I detest what you write, but I would give my life to make it possible for you to continue to write." Since the nation's birth, Mr. Bush, we have misquoted and even embellished that statement, but we have served ourselves well by subscribing to its essence.

Oddly, there are other words of Voltaire's that are more pertinent still just now:

"Think for yourselves," he wrote, "and let others enjoy the privilege to do so, too."

Apologize, sir, for even hinting at an America where a few have that privilege to think and the rest of us get yelled at by the president.

Anything else, Mr. Bush, is truly unacceptable.

6

A Textbook Definition
of Cowardice

September 25, 2006

Somebody once told me juxtaposition—not timing—was everything.

So here was former president Clinton, fresh from the second annual meeting of his extraordinary Global Initiative, wrapping up an interview with Tim Russert and laughing as he wagged a finger at me and saying with fake menace "and I'll be back for you." He left the room, to be escorted down the hallway to conduct the second of three promised interviews that day.

When the president got back thirty minutes later, he was not laughing. He was gesturing strongly to an aide, in shared anger. He asked my producers if we were ready to go, returned to give his staffer a few more instructions, then sat down and fixed his gaze on the floor in front of me. I got the signal from my producer and told him it was time. He sighed, lifted his gaze to mine, and smiled. And I knew I had witnessed not just the "compartmentalization" for which our forty-second president is famous, but also a kind of inner triumph over anger and dispute. Over what, I knew only that the previous interview had been with Chris Wallace of Fox News.

That interview, of course, was a sandbag job. Wallace had abrogated an agreement to spend at least half the interview discussing the Global Initiative, and instead almost immediately launched into not just an attack on Clinton for not "getting" Osama bin Laden, but an attack that employed two of the great con jobs of Fixed News—I'm sorry, Fox Noise. The question was based not on any facts about al-Qaeda or the Clinton administration, but rather on the just-telecast abomination *The Path to 9/11*. Transferring details from that right-wing fantasy of being able to blame Clinton for everything up to and including the disappearance of Judge Crater into a news interview, gave those falsehoods the patina of seeming legitimacy—the kind of verisimilitude that is sufficient for those who'd rather hear Clinton-bashing sophistry than the much more complicated facts.

But Wallace had also asked the question with utter gutlessness. He had not said, "Why didn't you kill bin Laden?" He had pinned the responsibility for the question on his viewers. He claimed so many of them had e-mailed him that he had no choice but to ask. One of our most prominent sportscasters at ESPN had mastered this preemptive buck-passing method ("Some people say") and had gradually worked his way out of the industry.

Not that I knew any of this at the time. I would have—and I bet you would have—leaned in to a more sympathetic interviewer and whispered, "Ask me about Fox News." But Mr. Clinton did not. In fact, the contemplative, statesmanlike answer he gave to one of my questions—considering that Wallace's partisan hit had to be still ringing in his ears—is the reason he was the president and the rest of us were not. I asked: "We've heard a lot about anyone who disagrees with the current administration's policy in Iraq or on the war on terror, or even disputes their facts or questions them, would be suffering from moral or intellectual confusion. The president talked about how in the world you could disagree with him, 'it's unacceptable to think' that we could ever be doing anything in any interrogation process that might be similar to what the terrorists do. When those of us worry about the future of the country and the past of the country, worry about our heritage, what we stand for, are we overreacting? Are we nuts? Are we exaggerating? Would you feel this is a threat?"

And President Clinton answered, "No—let me say, first of all, you know, on a lot of these issues I'm more close to where you are. I think what's the great disservice, though, that's been done here in the last few years is not that let's say the administration disagrees with you or me on whether there should be an Abu Ghraib or a Guantánamo or what the economic or social policies of America should be. The great disservice is the creation of the idea that if you disagree with the people that are in, you're somehow, you don't love your country and you can't be trusted to defend it. What we have to do is to get back to a point, to thinking in America and to promoting honest debate and honest differences, so that like, if you asked, and I would urge you to do this, if you interview somebody in the administration, no matter how much you disagree with them, don't be snide. Give them a straight-up chance to say how they disagree with you."

Slandered by ABC's *The Path to 9/11*. The victim of a broken agreement with Fox. Shivved by Chris Wallace. And he's reminding us not to be snide, to give the Bush administration a chance.

Oh, and there was one other juxtaposition Bill Clinton had to overcome to say that—a story I wouldn't hear until weeks later:

At the end of the Fox interview, Chris Wallace actually asked Clinton to sign an autograph.

Within hours, the administration and its water-carriers, desperate to shift any blame for 9/11 away from George W. Bush (even though he happened to have been president of the United States at the time), had converted the falsehoods of the three-card monte game that was the Wallace-Clinton interview into a series of parroting points.

And another Special Comment became necessary.

———

THE HEADLINES about them are, of course, entirely wrong.

It is not essential that a past president, bullied and sandbagged by a monkey posing as a newscaster, finally lashed back.

It is not important that the current president's portable public chorus has described his predecessor's tone as "crazed."

Our tone *should* be crazed. The nation's freedoms are under assault by an administration whose policies can do us as much damage as al-Qaeda; the nation's marketplace of ideas is being poisoned by a propaganda company so blatant that Tokyo Rose would've quit.

Nonetheless. The headline is this:

Bill Clinton did what almost none of us have done in five years.

He has spoken the truth about 9/11, and the current presidential administration.

"At least I tried," he said of his own efforts to capture or kill Osama bin Laden. "That's the difference in me and some, including all of the right-wingers who are attacking me now. They had eight months to try; they did not try. I tried."

Thus in his supposed emeritus years has Mr. Clinton taken forceful and triumphant action for honesty, and for us; action as vital and as courageous as any of his presidency; action as startling and as liberating, as any, by anyone, in these last five long years.

The Bush administration did not try to get Osama bin Laden before 9/11.

The Bush administration ignored all the evidence gathered by its predecessors.

The Bush administration did not understand the Daily Briefing entitled "Bin Laden Determined to Strike in U.S."

The Bush administration did not try.

Moreover, for the last five years, one month, and two weeks, the current administration, and in particular the president, has been given the greatest "pass" for incompetence and malfeasance in American history!

President Roosevelt was rightly blamed for ignoring the warning signs—some of them seventeen years old—before Pearl Harbor.

President Hoover was correctly blamed for—if not the Great Depression itself—then the disastrous economic steps he took in the immediate aftermath of the stock market crash.

Even President Lincoln assumed some measure of responsibility for the Civil War—though talk of Southern secession had begun as early as 1832.

But not this president.

To hear him bleat and whine and bully at nearly every opportunity, one would think someone else had been president on September 11, 2001—or the nearly eight months that preceded it.

That hardly reflects the honesty nor manliness we expect of the executive.

But if his own fitness to serve is of no true concern to him, perhaps we should simply sigh and keep our fingers crossed until a grown-up takes the job three Januarys from now.

Except for this.

After five years of skirting even the most inarguable of facts—that he was president on 9/11 and he must bear some responsibility for his, and our, unreadiness—Mr. Bush has now moved, unmistakably and without conscience or shame, toward rewriting history, and attempting to make the responsibility entirely Mr. Clinton's.

Of course he is not honest enough to do that directly.

As with all the other nefariousness and slime of this, our worst presidency since James Buchanan, he is having it done for him by proxy.

Thus the sandbag effort by Fox News on Friday afternoon.

Consider the timing: the very weekend the National Intelligence Estimate would be released and show the Iraq war to be the fraudulent failure it is—not a check on terror, but fertilizer for it.

The kind of proof of incompetence for which the administration and its hyenas at Fox need to find a diversion, in a scapegoat.

It was the kind of cheap trick which would get a journalist fired—but a propagandist promoted:

Promise to talk of charity and generosity, but instead launch into the lies and distortions with which the authoritarians among us attack the virtuous and reward the useless.

And don't even be professional enough to assume the responsibility for the slanders yourself; blame your audience for "e-mailing" you the question.

Mr. Clinton responded as you have seen.

He told the great truth untold about this administration's negligence, perhaps criminal negligence, about bin Laden.

He was brave.

Then again, Chris Wallace might be braver still. Had I in one moment surrendered all my credibility as a journalist and been irredeemably humiliated, as was he, I would have gone home and started a new career selling seeds by mail.

The smearing by proxy, of course, did not begin Friday afternoon.

Disney was first to sell out its corporate reputation, with *The Path to 9/11*. Of that company's crimes against truth one needs to say little. Simply put: Someone there enabled an authoritarian zealot to belch out Mr. Bush's new and improved history.

The basic plotline was this: Because he was distracted by the Monica Lewinsky scandal, Bill Clinton failed to prevent 9/11.

The most curious and in some ways the most infuriating aspect of this slapdash theory is that the right-wingers who have advocated it—who try to sneak it into our collective consciousness through entertainment, or who sandbag Mr. Clinton with it at news interviews—have simply skipped past its most glaring flaw:

Had it been true that Clinton had been distracted from the hunt for bin Laden in 1998 because of the Monica Lewinsky nonsense, why did these same people not applaud him for having bombed bin Laden's camps in Afghanistan and Sudan on August 20 of that year? For mentioning bin Laden by name as he did so?

That day, Republican senator Grams of Minnesota invoked the movie *Wag the Dog*.

Republican senator Coats of Indiana questioned Mr. Clinton's judgment.

Republican senator Ashcroft of Missouri—the future attorney general—echoed Coats.

Even Republican senator Arlen Specter questioned the timing.

And of course, were it true Clinton had been "distracted" by the Lewinsky witch hunt, who on earth conducted the Lewinsky witch hunt?

Who turned the political discourse of this nation on its head for two years?

Who corrupted the political media?

Who made it impossible for us to even bring back on the air the counterterrorism analysts like Dr. Richard Haass, and James Dunegan, who had warned, at this very hour, on this very network, in early 1998, of cells from the Middle East who sought to attack us, here?

Who preempted them in order to strangle us with the trivia that was "All Monica All the Time"?

Who distracted whom?

This is, of course, where—as is inevitable—Mr. Bush and his henchmen prove not quite as smart as they think they are.

The full responsibility for 9/11 is obviously shared by three administrations, possibly four.

But, Mr. Bush, if you are now trying to convince us by proxy that it's all about the distractions of 1998 and 1999, then you will have to face a startling fact that your minions may have hidden from you:

The distractions of 1998 and 1999, Mr. Bush, were carefully manufactured, and lovingly executed, not by Bill Clinton, but by the same people who got you elected president.

Thus, instead of some commendable acknowledgment that you were even in office on 9/11 and the lost months before it, we have your sleazy and sloppy rewriting of history, designed by somebody who evidently read the Orwell playbook too quickly.

Thus, instead of some explanation for the inertia of your first eight months in office, we are told that you have kept us "safe" ever since—a statement that might range anywhere from zero to one hundred percent true.

We have nothing but your word, and your word has long since ceased to mean anything.

And, of course, the one time you have ever given us specifics about what you have kept us safe from, Mr. Bush, you got the name of the supposedly targeted tower in Los Angeles wrong.

Thus was it left for the previous president to say what so many of us have felt, what so many of us have given you a pass for in the months and even the years after the attack:

You did not try.

You ignored the evidence gathered by your predecessor. You ignored the evidence gathered by your own people. Then, you blamed your predecessor.

That would be a textbook definition, Mr. Bush, of cowardice.

To enforce the lies of the present, it is necessary to erase the truths of the past. That was one of the great mechanical realities Eric Blair—writing as George Orwell—gave us in the book *1984*.

The great philosophical reality he gave us, Mr. Bush, may sound as familiar to you, as it has lately begun to sound familiar to me:

The Party seeks power entirely for its own sake. We are not interested in the good of others; we are interested solely in power . . .

Power is not a means; it is an end.

One does not establish a dictatorship to safeguard a revolution; one makes the revolution in order to establish the dictatorship.

The object of persecution, is persecution. The object of torture, is torture. The object of power . . . is power.

Earlier last Friday afternoon, before the Fox ambush, speaking in the far different context of the closing session of his remarkable Global Initiative, Mr. Clinton quoted Abraham Lincoln's State of the Union address from 1862:

"We must disenthrall ourselves."

Mr. Clinton did not quote the rest of Mr. Lincoln's sentence.

He might well have:

"We must disenthrall ourselves and then we shall save our country."

And so has Mr. Clinton helped us to disenthrall ourselves, and perhaps enabled us, even at this late and bleak date, to save our country.

The "free pass" has been withdrawn, Mr. Bush.

You did not act to prevent 9/11.

We do not know what you have done to prevent another 9/11.

You have failed us—then leveraged that failure to justify a purposeless war in Iraq which will have, all too soon, claimed more American lives than did 9/11.

You have failed us anew in Afghanistan.

And you have now tried to hide your failures by blaming your predecessor.

And now you exploit your failure, to rationalize brazen torture which doesn't work anyway; which only condemns our soldiers to waterboarding; which only humiliates our country further in the world; and which no true American would ever condone, let alone advocate.

And there it is, Mr. Bush: Are yours the actions of a true American?

7

On Lying

October 5, 2006

What made me hesitate in opening the envelope, I can't say for certain.

But I didn't recognize the return address, and my own was wrong in one specific detail the FBI still thinks I should leave out.

Maybe there was some instinct involved. With the September 25 defense of Bill Clinton at this point just about three hours past, we were now four Special Comments into the process (or five, depending on whether you count the brief bit about Bush trying to link the terms "al-Qaeda" and "media," on September 5). I had seen a lot of adulation and no little astonishment, so given the fractured state of our political discourse, I suppose deep down I was wondering where the hate was.

Anyway, I tore the edge of the dubious envelope slowly, far more slowly than all the stimuli hit me.

Grainy.

Shiny.

Powdery.

It was the letter inside that was grainy—some substance stuck to it.

Loose granules of some sort still in the envelope were shiny. And the powdery was the tiny puff of something that followed the tearing of the envelope itself.

And some of the grainy, shiny, powdery stuff was now on my finger-tips, and, unless I was a magician, in my lungs. The letter accompany-ing this little greeting was just barely visible, merely from the pressure my squeezed hand had exerted on the envelope: "America has enough demagogues," I remembered as I told the authorities later, and jotted some notes from inside the isolation room into which they trundled me. "Take some of your own medicine."

Could've been some other phrasing. Could've been those words exactly. I didn't bother to read it twice.

I got a plastic baggy from my kitchen and sealed it—the edge of the envelope that I'd torn away, still attached at the corner, and nearly all the contents intact.

But nearly, of course, only counts in horseshoes and hand grenades and threatening letters with white powder in them.

Honestly, it would be a couple of hours before I conceded to myself that there was even a one-in-a-thousand chance the powdery stuff might actually be anthrax. I'd covered the mechanics of the actual an-thrax poisonings of 2001 for CNN; I understood that anybody trying to handle anthrax as a weapon stood an excellent chance of killing them-selves long before they got their missive into a mailbox somewhere.

But right then, as I tried to keep my breathing under control, and call my girlfriend and not panic her out of moving from Los Angeles five days later into the very room into which the powder had spilled, two thoughts were predominant in my mind. The stuff certainly could've been something: shredded fiberglass or rat poison or sneez-ing powder or who-knows-what. Might not be fatal, might not even be scary, but it might have been mildly injurious.

More important, I'd waited until past midnight to open the mail that night. I had been "exposed" for ten minutes, and certainly if I showed any symptoms of anything even hours later, I could get treatment in time.

But at my apartment building, the mail was delivered around 2 P.M. What if there'd been a tear in the corner of that envelope? What, then, about the letter carrier? What, then, about the little old ladies who got their mail from the boxes around mine? What about the hardworking and friendly staff of what we all liked to call "New York's Highest-Priced Slum"?

If there was anything dangerous in there, they might all have been exposed to it ten hours earlier. Good grief, their time was just about up.

So I rather sheepishly did it. I called 911.

I'll spare you any further suspense (if any remains). The powder was detergent or drain cleaner or something. They would find the guy. They would videotape him mailing the envelope. They would discover that, though in his late thirties, he lived in his mom's basement and thought Ann Coulter, Laura Ingraham, and Katherine Harris were the three hottest women in America.

All that, however, was a long time in the future.

The police were not. They, and soon after, the FBI, arrived with startling rapidity. And they continued to arrive, in all shapes and sizes, in small groups and large, with the frequency and regularity and even comedy of the Marx Brothers' stateroom scene.

Within an hour they had filled the hallway outside my place and taken over a vacant apartment down the hall as a command post. And then all of a sudden they didn't want me inside my apartment any more.

Just a precaution, of course.

Like the Geiger counter was just a precaution.

And the Decon shower (that's decontamination, for you rookies).

And the Hazmat suit—which, it finally dawns on you at Hour Three or Four, seems to be made of the same stuff as FedEx packs.

Just a precaution.

Which is what, the eighteen or so officers assured me, my trip to the emergency room would be. I was almost certainly in no danger, but now this was a public health issue, and I really should go voluntarily, because otherwise they might have to, well, take me into protective custody and drag me there.

There were a lot of jokes, of course. Just like back in my L.A. days, about earthquakes. You were 99 percent kidding. The other 1 percent you didn't want to think about. But the joking helps. "Okay," said one officer as he gazed up and down my ill-fitting Hazmat costume. "Which movie do you look like you just stepped out of?" I was as stumped by the question as I was reassured by the impending punch line: "*Sleeper*! With Woody Allen! Are you ready to clone the nose?"

The precautions resumed: The ambulance. The vital signs, taken en route. The side door into the hospital. The chest X-ray. The Cipro. Everybody else wearing masks; some of them, shields.

Seriously, I'd love to attribute the fact that I wasn't scared to bravery. It really owed to logic: We know what to do for anthrax by now.

Those cops (and you're reminded anew: "New York's Finest" is neither a brand name nor an exaggeration) were as well trained as a football team during a kickoff. And who the hell would really count on my reaction to be fear and not anger? You don't like the Special Comments? Great. At least you could've paid attention to the clue I left in them: I am prepared to fight.

The only time I worried (about the continuing existence of me, anyway) was when they admitted me directly into an examining cubicle in the emergency room. Hell, I once waited two hours in a hospital in Queens after I ran headfirst into a parked subway train, and when they finally saw me they asked me what was wrong and I had used up all my patience and only the snideness was left: "Technically," I said, "I'm still bleeding to death."

So there I sat—in "Contact Isolation"—until the Hazmat team back at my apartment was satisfied that they hadn't found anything stronger than Mr. Clean, and until the good folks at Roosevelt Hospital could tell me that the X-rays and blood tests had come back and I seemed to be in better shape than at my last physical.

They finally wheeled me up to a private room, where they insisted I stay until at least the following afternoon. There was some back-and-forth about this with the City Department of Health: Quite understand-ably, they wanted not just the word of the Hazmat team and the hospital that there was no anthrax or poltergeist or whatever in my apartment or in me—they wanted paperwork. Finally, I talked the doctors into letting me go, with the promise that I'd pop a Cipro at the first sign of—well, of anything, really—and rush back to the comfort of their Contact Isolation.

Casualties: Lost a night's sleep. Two dozen cops and investigators who could've been chasing somebody wasted their time. Some very good docs got to practice treating a guy who wasn't sick. Everything I was wearing at the time I opened the envelope was irradiated, includ-ing what is now an extremely rare "Mobile ESPN" phone, my wallet, my shoes, and my photo ID (gotta admit it's been an unbeatable excuse when people have asked me for it: "Sorry, the FBI burned it").

One of the detectives was nice enough to bring over a suit from my apartment so I had something to walk home in before taking a quick nap and going on the air that night with *Countdown.* Not a word about the incident, of course, because, as the FBI guys pointed out, as tempting as it was to tell the story the way I have here, from notes written in that Contact Isolation room that night, doing so would only assure the sender that he'd accomplished his sick mission, and that he had my address. They couldn't stop me from revealing it had hap-pened ("Jeez," said one of the FBI guys, "if I had a newscast I'd do the whole show about it"), but in a very clear way, in revealing it, I would be helping a domestic terrorist.

So that was the story, on which I sat, and was going to, forever if necessary.

And then the next day's product of the tiny minds at the *New York Post* hit the street, and an act of honest-to-goodness homegrown terrorism was reduced to a guffaw by morons for morons in its infamous (and remarkably incorrect) gossip page:

> Keith Olbermann flipped out when he opened his home mail yesterday.
>
> The acerbic host of "Countdown with Keith Olbermann" was terrified when he opened a suspicious-looking letter with a California postmark and a batch of white powder poured out. A note inside warned Olbermann, who's a frequent critic of President Bush's policies, that it was payback for some of his on-air shtick. The caustic commentator panicked and frantically called 911 at about 12:30 a.m., sources told The Post's Philip Messing. An NYPD Haz-Mat unit rushed to Olbermann's pad on Central Park South, but preliminary tests indicated the substance was harmless soap powder. However, that wasn't enough to satisfy Olbermann, who insisted on a checkup. He asked to be taken to St. Luke's Hospital, where doctors looked him over and sent him home.
>
> Whether they gave him a lollipop on the way out isn't known. Olbermann had no comment.

Of course I didn't. The Post never called me, nor did MSNBC, nor, apparently, the FBI or the NYPD. If they had, they would've been advised that, yes, there had been an incident, but, oh, by the way, the local representatives of the federal government (G. W. Bush, Proprietor) had asked everybody to keep it quiet so as not to provide the perpetrator with a return receipt. Especially considering that the guy had sent similar letters to Jon Stewart, David Letterman, and Sumner Redstone (Letterman's ultimate boss).

Some woman from the Post did come over to the apartment to ask my neighbors about things—scaring the hell out of a couple of them—until she was warned off the property and hightailed it like the little devil's minion she was.

The *Post,* having come down on the side of the terrorists, and hav-ing gotten resultingly spanked not just on my show, but also in the vast majority of the right-wing blogs, has not mentioned the incident since. It has reverted to its specialty: some totally inaccurate and, more im-portant from its bosses' viewpoints, really dull attacks on me. They are certainly in the same ethical league as the guy with the powder, but lack his creativity or spark.

Things got back to normal relatively quickly. I had a war wound. The girlfriend moved in anyway (and braved a second envelope before the nitwitted sender got himself caught). I went on David Letterman's show the following Tuesday (and he asked about neither the letter nor the Special Comments).

And a few hours before I went out onto his Ed Sullivan Theater stage—far colder than even Dave jokes about—President Bush, for the second time in as many days, told an audience that the Democrats didn't want the government listening "to the conversations of terrorists."

Well. Fake-Anthrax-Letter received and figuratively still in my pocket, I thought: I now have a little more firsthand experience with terrorism than Mr. Bush does. And I certainly have a whole lot more understanding of the topic. I sat down at my keyboard intent on leaving him and his enablers feeling as cold as Letterman's stage.

WHILE THE LEADERSHIP in Congress has self-destructed over the reve-lations of an unmatched, and unrelieved, march through a cesspool; while the leadership inside the White House has self-destructed over the revelations of a book with a glowing red cover* . . . the president of the United States—unbowed, undeterred, and unconnected to reality—has continued his extraordinary trek through our country rooting out the enemies of freedom: the Democrats.

*Bob Woodward's *State of Denial: Bush at War, Part III.*

Yesterday at a fundraiser for an Arizona congressman, Mr. Bush claimed, "One hundred seventy-seven of the opposition party said, 'You know, we don't think we ought to be listening to the conversations of terrorists.'"

The hell they did.

One hundred seventy-seven Democrats opposed the president's seizure of another part of the Constitution.

Not even the White House press office could actually name a single Democrat who had ever said the government shouldn't be listening to the conversations of terrorists.

President Bush hears what he wants.

Tuesday, at another fundraiser in California, he had said, "Democrats take a law enforcement approach to terrorism. That means America will wait until we're attacked again before we respond."

Mr. Bush fabricated that, too.

And evidently he has begun to fancy himself a mind reader.

"If you listen closely to some of the leaders of the Democratic Party," the president said at another fundraiser Monday in Nevada, "it sounds like they think the best way to protect the American people is—wait until we're attacked again."

The president doesn't just hear what he wants. He hears things that only he can hear.

It defies belief that this president and his administration could continue to find new, unexplored political gutters into which they could wallow.

Yet they do.

It is startling enough that such things could be said out loud by any president of this nation. Rhetorically, it is about an inch short of Mr. Bush accusing Democratic leaders, Democrats, the majority of Americans who disagree with his policies, of treason.

But it is the context that truly makes the head spin.

Just twenty-five days ago, on the fifth anniversary of the 9/11 attacks, this same man spoke to this nation and insisted, "We must put aside our differences and work together to meet the test that history has given us."

Mr. Bush, this is a test you have already failed.

If your commitment to "put aside differences and work together" is replaced in the span of just three weeks by claiming your political opponents prefer to wait to see this country attacked again, and by spewing fabrications about what they've said, then the questions your critics need to be asking are no longer about your policies.

They are, instead, solemn and even terrible questions about your fitness to fulfill the responsibilities of your office.

No Democrat, sir, has ever said anything approaching the suggestion that the best means of self-defense is to "wait until we're attacked again."

No critic, no commentator, no reluctant Republican in the Senate has ever said anything that any responsible person could even have exaggerated into the slander you spoke in Nevada on Monday night, nor the slander you spoke in California on Tuesday, nor the slander you spoke in Arizona on Wednesday . . . nor whatever is next.

You have dishonored your party, sir; you have dishonored your supporters; you have dishonored yourself.

But tonight the stark question we must face is—why?

Why has the ferocity of your venom against the Democrats now exceeded the ferocity of your venom against the terrorists?

Why have you chosen to go down in history as the president who made things up?

In less than one month you have gone from a flawed call to unity to this clarion call to hatred of Americans by Americans. If this is not simply the most shameless example of the rhetoric of political hackery, then it would have to be the cry of a leader crumbling under the weight of his own lies.

We have, of course, survived all manner of political hackery, of every shape, size, and party. We will have to suffer it for as long as the republic stands. But the premise of a president who comes across as a compulsive liar is nothing less than terrifying.

A president who since 9/11 will not listen, is not listening—and thanks to Bob Woodward's most recent account, evidently has never listened.

A president who since 9/11 so hates or fears other Americans that he accuses them of advocating deliberate inaction in the face of the enemy.

A president who since 9/11 has savaged the very freedoms he claims to be protecting from attack—attack by terrorists, or by Democrats, or by both; it is now impossible to find a consistent thread of logic as to who Mr. Bush believes the enemy is.

But if we know one thing for certain about Mr. Bush, it is this: This president—in his bullying of the Senate last month and in his slandering of the Democrats this month—has shown us that he believes whoever the enemies are, they are hiding themselves inside a dangerous cloak called the Constitution of the United States of America.

How often do we find priceless truth in the unlikeliest of places?

I tonight quote not Jefferson nor Voltaire, but *Cigar Aficionado* magazine.

On September 11, 2003, the editor of that publication interviewed General Tommy Franks, at that point just retired from his post as commander in chief of U.S. Central Command—of CENTCOM.

And amid his quaint defenses of the then nagging absence of weapons of mass destruction in Iraq, or the continuing freedom of Osama bin Laden, General Franks said some of the most profound words of this generation.

He spoke of "the worst thing that can happen" to this country:

First, a "massive casualty-producing event somewhere in the Western World—it may be in the United States of America." Then, the general continued, "the Western World, the free world, loses what it cherishes most, and that is freedom and liberty we've seen for a couple of hundred years, in this grand experiment that we call democracy."

It was this super-patriotic warrior's fear that we would lose that most cherished liberty because of another attack, one—again quoting General Franks—"that causes our population to question our own Constitution and to begin to militarize our country in order to avoid a repeat of another mass-casualty-producing event. Which, in fact, then begins to potentially unravel the fabric of our Constitution."

And here we are, the fabric of our Constitution being unraveled anyway.

Habeas corpus neutered; the rights of self-defense now as malleable and impermanent as clay; a president stifling all critics by every means available, and, when he runs out of those, by simply lying about what they said or felt.

And all this even without the dreaded attack.

General Franks, like all of us, loves this country, and believes not just in its values, but in its continuity.

He has been trained to look for threats to that continuity from without.

He has, perhaps, been as naïve as the rest of us, in failing to keep close enough vigil on the threats to that continuity from within.

Secretary of State Rice first cannot remember urgent cautionary meetings with counterterrorism officials before 9/11. Then, within hours of this lie, her spokesman confirms the meetings in question. Then she dismisses those meetings as nothing new—yet insists she wanted the same cautions expressed to Secretaries Ashcroft and Rumsfeld.

Mr. Rumsfeld, meantime, has been unable to accept the most logical and simple influence of the most noble and neutral of advisers. He and his employer insist they rely on "the generals in the field." But dozens of those generals have now come forward to say how their words, their experiences, have been ignored.

And, of course, inherent in the Pentagon's war-making functions is the regulation of presidential war lust.

Enacting that regulation should include everything up to symbolically wrestling the chief executive to the floor.

Yet—and it is Pentagon transcripts that now tell us this—evidently Mr. Rumsfeld's strongest check on Mr. Bush's ambitions was to get somebody to excise the phrase "Mission Accomplished" out of the infamous Air Force carrier speech of May 1, 2003, even while the same empty words hung on a banner over the president's shoulder.

And the vice president is a chilling figure, still unable, it seems, to accept the conclusions of his own party's leaders in the Senate, that the foundations of his public position are made out of sand.

There were no weapons of mass destruction in Iraq.

But he still says so.

There was no link between Saddam Hussein and al-Qaeda.

But he still says so.

And thus, gripping firmly these figments of his own imagination, Mr. Cheney lives on, in defiance, and spreads—around him and before him—darkness, like some contagion of fear.

They are never wrong, and they never regret—admirable in a French torch singer, cataclysmic in an American leader.

Thus the sickening attempt to blame the Foley scandal on the negligence of others or "the Clinton era"—even though the Foley scandal began before the Lewinsky scandal.

Thus last month's enraged attacks on this administration's predecessors about Osama bin Laden—a projection of their own negligence in the immediate months before 9/11.

Thus the terrifying attempt to hamstring the fundament of our freedom—the Constitution—a triumph for al-Qaeda which the terrorists could not hope to achieve with a hundred 9/11s.

And thus, worst of all perhaps, these newest lies by President Bush about Democrats choosing to await another attack and not listen to the conversations of terrorists.

It is the terror and the guilt within your own heart, Mr. Bush, that you redirect at others who simply wish for you to temper your certainty with counsel.

It is the failure and the incompetence within your own memory, Mr. Bush, that leads you to demonize those who might merely quote to you the pleadings of Oliver Cromwell: "I beseech you, in the bowels of Christ, think it possible you may be mistaken."

It is not the Democrats whose inaction in the face of the enemy you fear, sir.

It is your own—before 9/11, and (and you alone know this) perhaps afterward.

Mr. President, these new lies go to the heart of what it is that you truly wish to preserve.

It is not our freedom, nor our country—your actions against the Constitution give irrefutable proof of that.

You want to preserve a political party's power. And obviously you'll sell this country out to do it.

These are lies about the Democrats, piled atop lies about Iraq, which were piled atop lies about your preparations for al-Qaeda.

To you, perhaps, they feel like the weight of a million centuries—as crushing, as immovable.

They are not.

If you add more lies to them, you cannot free yourself, and us, from them.

But if you stop—if you stop fabricating quotes, and building straw men, and inspiring those around you to do the same—you may yet liberate yourself and this nation.

Please, sir, do not throw this country's principles away because your lies have made it such that you can no longer differentiate between the terrorists and the critics.

8

"The Beginning of the End of America"

October 18, 2006

I wrote this Special Comment in response to one of the sorrier moments in our recent history. After all the discussion leading up to the Military Commissions Act, designed to set up commissions to try detainees, you would have thought the actual law would have put some kind of check on the Bush administration's excesses. In fact, it did the opposite, codifying them legally. Among its notable effects was to strip detainees of their right to challenge their detention (habeas corpus); give the president the power to detain anyone, U.S. citizen or not, indefinitely; allow the president to determine the meaning and application of the Geneva Conventions; and strip courts of their role in hearing challenges to that interpretation. It also gave U.S. officials immunity from prosecution for torturing detainees who were captured before the end of 2005.

WE HAVE LIVED as if in a trance.

We have lived as people in fear.

And now—our rights and our freedoms in peril—we slowly awaken to learn that we have been afraid of the wrong thing.

Therefore, tonight have we truly become the inheritors of our American legacy. For on this first full day that the Military Commissions Act is in force, we now face what our ancestors faced at other times of exaggerated crisis and melodramatic fearmongering:

A government more dangerous to our liberty than is the enemy it claims to protect us from.

We have been here before—and we have been here before, led here by men better and wiser and nobler than George W. Bush.

We have been here when President John Adams insisted that the Alien and Sedition Acts were necessary to save American lives, only to watch him use those acts to jail newspaper editors.

American newspaper editors, in American jails, for things they wrote about America.

We have been here when President Woodrow Wilson insisted that the Espionage Act was necessary to save American lives, only to watch him use that act to prosecute two thousand Americans, especially those he disparaged as "hyphenated Americans," most of whom were guilty only of advocating peace in a time of war.

American public speakers, in American jails, for things they said about America.

And we have been here when President Franklin D. Roosevelt insisted that Executive Order 9066 was necessary to save American lives, only to watch him use that order to imprison and pauperize 110,000 Americans while his man in charge, General DeWitt, told Congress: "It makes no difference whether he is an American citizen—he is still a Japanese."

American citizens, in American camps, for something they neither wrote nor said nor did, but for the choices they or their ancestors had made about coming to America.

Each of these actions was undertaken for the most vital, the most urgent, the most inescapable of reasons.

And each was a betrayal of that for which the president who advocated them claimed to be fighting.

Adams and his party were swept from office, and the Alien and Sedition Acts erased.

Many of the very people Wilson silenced survived him, and one of them even ran to succeed him, and got 900,000 votes, though his presidential campaign was conducted entirely from his jail cell.

And Roosevelt's internment of the Japanese was not merely the worst blight on his record, but it would necessitate a formal apology from the government of the United States to the citizens of the United States whose lives it ruined.

The most vital, the most urgent, the most inescapable of reasons.

In times of fright, we have been only human. We have let Roosevelt's "fear of fear itself" overtake us.

We have listened to the little voice inside that has said, "The wolf is at the door; this will be temporary; this will be precise; this too shall pass."

We have accepted that the only way to stop the terrorists is to let the government become just a little bit like the terrorists.

Just the way we once accepted that the only way to stop the Soviets was to let the government become just a little bit like the Soviets.

Or substitute the Japanese.

Or the Germans.

Or the Socialists.

Or the Anarchists, or the Immigrants, or the British, or the Aliens.

The most vital, the most urgent, the most inescapable of reasons.

And always, always wrong.

"With the distance of history, the questions will be narrowed and few: Did this generation of Americans take the threat seriously, and did we do what it takes to defeat that threat?"

Wise words. And ironic ones, Mr. Bush.

Your own, of course, yesterday, in signing the Military Commissions Act.

You spoke so much more than you know, sir.

Sadly—of course—the distance of history will recognize that the threat this generation of Americans needed to take seriously was you.

We have a long and painful history of ignoring the prophecy attributed to Benjamin Franklin that "those who would give up essential liberty to purchase a little temporary safety, deserve neither liberty nor safety."

But even within this history we have not before codified the poisoning of habeas corpus, that wellspring of protection from which all essential liberties flow.

You, sir, have now befouled that spring.

You, sir, have now given us chaos and called it order.

You, sir, have now imposed subjugation and called it freedom.

For the most vital, the most urgent, the most inescapable of reasons.

And—again, Mr. Bush—all of them wrong.

We have handed a blank check drawn against our freedom to a man who has said it is unacceptable to compare anything this country has ever done to anything the terrorists have ever done.

We have handed a blank check drawn against our freedom to a man who has insisted again that "the United States does not torture. It's against our laws and it's against our values," and who has said it with a straight face while the pictures from Abu Ghraib Prison and the stories of waterboarding figuratively fade in and out around him.

We have handed a blank check drawn against our freedom to a man who may now, if he so decides, declare not merely any non-American citizens "unlawful enemy combatants" and ship them somewhere—anywhere—but may now, if he so decides, declare you an "unlawful enemy combatant" and ship you somewhere—anywhere.

And if you think this hyperbole or hysteria, ask the newspaper editors when John Adams was president or the pacifists when Woodrow Wilson was president or the Japanese at Manzanar when Franklin Roosevelt was president.

And if you somehow think habeas corpus has not been suspended for American citizens but only for everybody else, ask yourself this: If you are pulled off the street tomorrow, and they call you an alien or an undocumented immigrant or an "unlawful enemy combatant"—exactly how are you going to convince them to give you a court hearing to prove you are not? Do you think this attorney general is going to help you?

This president now has his blank check.

He lied to get it.

He lied as he received it.

Is there any reason to even hope he has not lied about how he intends to use it nor who he intends to use it against?

"These military commissions will provide a fair trial," you told us yesterday, Mr. Bush, "in which the accused are presumed innocent, have access to an attorney, and can hear all the evidence against them."

"Presumed innocent," Mr. Bush?

The very piece of paper you signed as you said that allows for the detainees to be abused up to the point just before they sustain "serious mental and physical trauma" in the hope of getting them to incriminate themselves and may no longer even invoke the Geneva Conventions in their own defense.

"Access to an attorney," Mr. Bush?

Lieutenant Commander Charles Swift said on this program, sir, and to the Supreme Court, that he was only granted access to his detainee defendant on the promise that the detainee would plead guilty.

"Hearing all the evidence," Mr. Bush?

The Military Commissions Act specifically permits the introduction of classified evidence not made available to the defense.

Your words are lies, sir. They are lies that imperil us all.

"One of the terrorists believed to have planned the 9/11 attacks," you told us yesterday, "said he hoped the attacks would be the beginning of the end of America."

That terrorist, sir, could only hope. Not his actions, nor the actions of a ceaseless line of terrorists real or imagined, could measure up to what you have wrought.

Habeas corpus? Gone.

The Geneva Conventions? Optional.

The moral force we shined outwards to the world as an eternal beacon, and inward at ourselves as an eternal protection? Snuffed out.

These things you have done, Mr. Bush—*they* would be "the beginning of the end of America."

And did it even occur to you once, sir—somewhere in amidst those eight separate, gruesome, intentional, terroristic invocations of the horrors of 9/11—that with only a little further shift in this world we now know—just a touch more repudiation of all of that for which our patriots died—did it ever occur to you once that in just twenty-seven months and two days from now, when you leave office, some irresponsible future president and a "competent tribunal" of lackeys would be entitled, by the actions of your own hand, to declare the status of "unlawful enemy combatant" for—and convene a military commission to try—not John Walker Lindh, but George Walker Bush?

For the most vital, the most urgent, the most inescapable of reasons. And doubtless, sir, all of them—as always—wrong.

9

Advertising Terrorism

October 23, 2006

The Bush administration and its proxies have few peers in the use of fear as a political tool, particularly when they're attempting to divert public attention from their lamentable performance. A Republican National Committee television ad, yet one more desperate attempt to stave off midterm defeat, offered another neat example of this. The non-partisan watchdog site Factcheck.org, in a quietly scathing review of the ad, rightly pointed out that it was an "appeal to fear more than reason."

TONIGHT, a Special Comment on the advertising of terrorism—the commercial you have already seen.

It is a distillation of everything this administration and the party in power have tried to do these last five years and six weeks.

It is from the Republican National Committee.

It shows images of Osama bin Laden and Ayman al-Zawahiri.

It offers quotes from them—all as a clock ticks ominously in the background.

It concludes with what Zawahiri may or may not have said to a Pakistani journalist as long ago as 2001: his dubious claim that he had purchased "suitcase bombs."

The quotation is followed (by sheer coincidence, no doubt) by an image of a massive explosion.

"These are the stakes" appears on the screen, quoting exactly from Lyndon Johnson's infamous nuclear scare commercial from 1964.

"Vote—November 7th."

There is a cheap *Texas Chainsaw Massacre* quality to the whole thing, and it also serves to immediately call to mind the occasions when President Bush dismissed Osama bin Laden as somebody he didn't think about—except, obviously, when elections were near.

Frankly, a lot of people seeing that commercial for the first time have laughed out loud.

But not everyone. And therein lies the true threat to this country.

The dictionary definition of the word "terrorize" is simple and not open to misinterpretation: "To fill or overpower with terror; terrify. To coerce by intimidation or fear."

Note, please, that the words "violence" and "death" are missing from that definition. The key to terror, the key to terrorism, is not the act, but the fear of the act.

That is why bin Laden and his deputies and his imitators are forever putting together videotaped statements and releasing virtual infomercials with dire threats and heart-stopping warnings.

But why is the Republican Party imitating them?

Bin Laden puts out what amounts to a commercial of fear; the Republicans put out what is unmistakable as a commercial of fear.

The Republicans are paying to have the messages of bin Laden and the others broadcast into your home. Only the Republicans have a bigger bankroll.

When, last week, the CNN network ran video of an insurgent in Iraq, evidently stalking and killing an American soldier, the chairman of the

House Armed Services Committee, Mr. Hunter, Republican of California, branded that channel "the publicist for an enemy propaganda film" and that CNN used it "to sell commercials."

Another California Republican, Representative Brian Bilbray, called the video "nothing short of a terrorist snuff film."

If so, Mr. Bilbray, then what in the hell is your party's new advertisement?

And Mr. Hunter, CNN using the video to "sell commercials"?

Commercials!

You have adopted bin Laden and Zawahiri as spokesmen for the Republican National Committee!

"To fill or overpower with terror; terrify. To coerce by intimidation or fear." By this definition, the people who put these videos together—first the terrorists and then the administration, whose shared goal is to scare you into panicking instead of thinking—they are the ones terrorizing you.

By this definition, the leading terrorist group in this world right now is al-Qaeda.

But the leading terrorist group in this country right now is the Republican Party.

Eleven presidents ago, a chief executive reassured us that "we have nothing to fear but fear itself."

His distant successor has wasted his administration insisting that there is nothing we can *have* but fear itself.

The vice president, as recently as this month, was caught campaigning with the phrase "mass death in the United States." Four years ago it was the now secretary of state, Dr. Rice, rationalizing Iraq with "We don't want the smoking gun to be a mushroom cloud." Days later Mr. Bush himself told an audience that "we cannot wait for the final proof, the smoking gun, that could come in the form of a mushroom cloud." And now we have this cheesy commercial, complete with images of a faked mushroom cloud and implications of "mass death in America."

This administration has derived benefit and power from terrorizing the very people it claims to be protecting from terror.

It may be the oldest trick in the political book: Scare people into believing they are in danger and that only you can save them.

Lyndon Johnson used it to bury Barry Goldwater.

Joe McCarthy leaped from obscurity on its back.

And now the legacy has come to President George Bush.

Of course, the gruel of fear is getting thinner and thinner, is it not, Mr. President? And thus more and more of it needs to be made out of less and less actual terror.

After last week's embarrassing Internet hoax about "dirty bombs" at football stadiums, the one your Department of Homeland Security immediately disseminated to the public, a self-described "former CIA operative" named Wayne Simmons cited the fiasco as "the, and I mean the, perfect example of the president's Military Commissions Act of 2006 and the NSA terrorist eavesdropping program—how vital they are."

Frank Gaffney, once a respected assistant secretary of defense and now the president of something called the Center for Security Policy, added, "One of the things that I hope Americans take away from this is not only that they're gunning for us not just in a place like Iraq—but truly, worldwide."

Of course, the "they" to which Mr. Gaffney referred turned out to be a lone twenty-year-old grocery bagger from Wisconsin named Jake— a kid, trying to one-up some other loser in an Internet game of chicken. His "threat" referenced seven football stadiums at which dirty bombs were to be exploded yesterday. It began with the one in New York City— even though there isn't one in New York City. And though the attacks were supposed to be simultaneous, four of the games were scheduled to start at 1 P.M. Eastern time and the others at 4 P.M. Eastern time.

Moreover, the kid said he'd posted the identical message on forty websites since September. We caught him in "merely" about six weeks, even though the only way he could have been less subtle, less stealthy, and less of a threat was if he'd bought an advertisement on the Super Bowl broadcast.

Mr. Bush, this is the—what?—hundredth plot your people have revealed that turned out to be some nonsensical misunderstanding, or the fabrications of somebody hoping to talk his way off a waterboard in Eastern Europe?

If, Mr. President, this is the kind of crack work that your new ad implies that only you and not the Democrats can do, you, sir, need to pull over and ask for directions.

The real question of course, Mr. Bush, is why did your Department of Homeland Security even release this information in the first place? It was never a serious threat. Even the first news accounts quoted a Homeland spokesman as admitting "strong skepticism"—the kind of strong skepticism which most government agencies address *before* telling the public, not afterwards.

So that leaves two options, Mr. President.

The first option: You and your Department of Homeland Security don't have the slightest idea what you're doing. Thus, contrary to your flip-flopping between saying "We're safe" and saying "But we're not safe enough," and contrary to the vice president's swaggering pronouncements about the lack of another attack since 9/11, the last five years has been just an accident.

Or there's the second option: Your political operatives leaked this nonsense for the same reason your political operatives put out that commercial—to scare the gullible.

Obviously the correct answer, Mr. Bush, is "all of the above."

There are some of us who could forgive you for trying to run your candidates on the coattails of the Grim Reaper, for reducing your party's existence to "Death and Attacks Us."

It's cynical and barbaric.

But, after all, it may be merely the natural extension of the gutter politics to which you have subscribed since you sidled over from baseball and the business world of other people's money.

But to forgive you for terrorizing us, we would have to believe you somehow competent in keeping others from doing so.

Yet, last week, construction workers repairing a subway line in New York City were cleaning out an abandoned manhole on the edge of the World Trade Center site when they stumbled onto the impossible: human remains from 9/11.

Bones and fragments. Eighty of them. Some as much as a foot long.

The victims had been lying, literally in the gutter, for five years and five weeks.

The families and friends of each of the 2,749 dead—who had been grimly told in May of 2002 that there were no more remains to be found—were struck anew as if the terrorism of that day had just happened again.

And over the weekend they've found still more remains.

And now this week will be spent looking in places that should have already been looked at a thousand times five years ago.

For all the victims in New York, Mr. Bush—the living and the dead—it's a touch of 9/11 all over again.

And the mayor of this city, who called off the search four and a half years ago, is a Republican.

The governor of this state with whom he conferred is a Republican.

The House of Representatives, Republican.

The Senate, Republican.

The president, Republican.

And yet you can actually claim that you and you alone can protect us from terrorism?

You can't even recover our dead from the battlefield—the battlefield in an American city—when we've given you five years and unlimited funds to do so!

While signing a Military Commissions Act so monstrous that it has been criticized by even the John Birch Society, you told us, Mr. Bush, "There is nothing we can do to bring back the men and women lost on September 11, 2001. Yet we'll always honor their memory, and we will never forget the way they were taken from us."

Except, of course, for the ones who've been lying under a manhole cover for five years.

Setting aside the fact that your government has done nothing else for those five years but pat yourselves on the back about terror while waging pointless war on the wrong enemy in Iraq and waging war on the cherished freedoms in America, just on this subject of counterterrorism, sir, yours is the least competent government, in time of crisis, in this country's history!

"These are the stakes," indeed, Mr. President.

You do not know what you are doing.

And the commercial—the one about which Zawahiri might say, "Hey, pretty good—we love your choice of font style"?

All that need further be said is to add three words to Shakespeare:

Mr. President, you, and that advertisement of terror, are full of sound and fury—signifying (and competent at) nothing.

10

Bush Owes the Troops
an Apology, Not Kerry

November 1, 2006

On October 30, 2006, a mere eight days before the midterm elections, John Kerry gave desperate Republicans the opportunity they had been looking for. At a rally in California, as he repeatedly zinged the president with one-liners, he connected the president's stupidity and lack of intellectual curiosity with his most notable fiasco: "You know, education, if you make the most of it, you study hard, you do your homework and you make an effort to be smart, you can do well. If you don't, you get stuck in Iraq." The president, his staff, and several notable Republican politicians immediately took the opportunity to smear Kerry by suggesting that his comments were aimed at the troops, even though it was obvious he was referring to the president. In case the point wasn't clear, the White House also released the president's annual Veterans Day proclamation in support of the armed forces— a week and a half before the holiday.

ON THE TWENTY-SECOND of May, 1856, as the deteriorating American political system veered toward the edge of the cliff, U.S. representative

Preston Brooks of South Carolina shuffled into the Senate of this nation, his leg stiff from an old dueling injury, supported by a cane. And he looked for the familiar figure of the prominent senator from Massachusetts, Charles Sumner.

Brooks found Sumner at his desk, mailing out copies of a speech he had delivered three days earlier—a speech against slavery.

The congressman matter-of-factly raised his walking stick in midair and smashed its metal point across the senator's head.

Congressman Brooks hit his victim repeatedly. Senator Sumner somehow got to his feet and tried to flee. Brooks chased him and delivered untold blows to Sumner's head. Even though Sumner lay unconscious and bleeding on the Senate floor, Brooks finally stopped beating him only because his cane finally broke.

Others will cite John Brown's attack on the arsenal at Harpers Ferry as the exact point after which the Civil War became inevitable.

In point of fact, it might have been the moment, not when Brooks broke his cane over the prostrate body of Senator Sumner—but when voters in Brooks's district started sending him new canes.

Tonight, we almost wonder to whom President Bush will send the next new cane.

There is tonight no political division in this country that he and his party will not exploit, nor have not exploited; no anxiety that he and his party will not inflame. There is no line this president has not crossed—nor will not cross—to keep one political party in power.

He has spread any and every fear among us in a desperate effort to avoid that which he most fears—some check, some balance against what has become not an imperial, but a unilateral presidency.

And now it is evident that it no longer matters to him whether that effort to avoid the judgment of the people is subtle and nuanced or laughably transparent.

Senator John Kerry called him out Monday.

He did it two years too late. He had been too cordial—just as Vice

President Gore had been too cordial in 2000, just as millions of us have been too cordial ever since.

Senator Kerry, as you well know, spoke at a college in Southern California. With bitter humor he told the students that he had been in Texas the day before, that President Bush used to live in that state, but that now he lives in the state of denial.

He said the trip had reminded him about the value of education— that "if you make the most of it, you study hard, you do your homework, and you make an effort to be smart, you can do well. If you don't, you get stuck in Iraq."

The senator, in essence, called Mr. Bush stupid.

The context was unmistakable. Texas. The state of denial. Stuck in Iraq. No interpretation required.

And Mr. Bush and his minions responded by appearing to be too stupid to realize that they had been called stupid.

They demanded Kerry apologize to the troops in Iraq.

And so he now has.

That phrase—"appearing to be too stupid"—is used deliberately, Mr. Bush.

Because there are only three possibilities here.

One, sir, is that you are far more stupid than the worst of your critics have suggested; that you could not follow the construction of a simple sentence; that you could not recognize your own life story when it was deftly summarized; that you could not perceive it was the sad ledger of your presidency that was being recounted.

This, of course, compliments you, Mr. Bush, because even those who do not "make the most of it," who do not "study hard," who do not "do their homework," and who do not "make an effort to be smart" might still just be stupid, but honest.

No, the first option, sir, is at best improbable. You are not honest.

The second option is that you and those who work for you deliberately twisted what Senator Kerry said to fit your political template; that

you decided to take advantage of it, to once again pretend that the attacks, solely about your own incompetence, were in fact attacks on the
troops or even on the nation itself.

The third possibility is, obviously, the nightmare scenario: that the
first two options are in some way conflated. That it is both politically
convenient for you and personally satisfying to you, to confuse yourself
with the country for which, sir, you work.

A brief reminder, Mr. Bush: You are not the United States of America.

You are merely a politician whose entire legacy will have been a willingness to make anything political; to have, in this case, refused to acknowledge that the insult wasn't about the troops, and that the insult
was not even truly about you either—that the insult, in fact, *is* you.

So now John Kerry has apologized to the troops—apologized for the
Republicans' deliberate distortions.

Thus, the president will now begin the apologies *he* owes our troops,
right?

This president must apologize to the troops for having suggested, six
weeks ago, that the chaos in Iraq, the death and the carnage, the slaugh-
tered Iraqi civilians and the dead American service personnel, will, to
history, "look like just a comma."

This president must apologize to the troops because the intelligence
he claims led us into Iraq proved to be undeniably and irredeemably
wrong.

This president must apologize to the troops for having laughed about
the failure of that intelligence at a banquet while our troops were in
harm's way.

This president must apologize to the troops because the streets of
Iraq were not strewn with flowers and its residents did not greet them as
liberators.

This president must apologize to the troops because his administration ran out of "plan" after barely two months.

This president must apologize to the troops for getting 2,815 of them killed.

This president must apologize to the troops for getting this country into a war without a clue.

And Mr. Bush owes us an apology for this destructive and omnivorous presidency.

We will not receive them, of course. This president never apologizes.

Not to the troops.

Not to the people.

Nor will those henchmen who have echoed him.

In calling him a "stuffed suit," Senator Kerry was wrong about the press secretary. Mr. Snow's words and conduct, falsely earnest and earnestly false, suggest he is not "stuffed," he is inflated.

And in leaving him out of the equation, Senator Kerry gave an unwarranted pass to his old friend Senator John McCain, who should be ashamed of himself tonight. He rolled over and pretended Kerry had said what he obviously had not.

Only the symbolic stick he broke over Kerry's head came in a context even more disturbing. Mr. McCain demanded the apology while electioneering for a Republican congressional candidate in Illinois.

He was speaking of how often he had been to Walter Reed Hospital to see the wounded Iraq veterans, of how "many of them have lost limbs." He said all this while demanding that the voters of Illinois reject a candidate who is not only a wounded Iraq veteran, but who lost two limbs there, Tammy Duckworth.

Support some of the wounded veterans. But bad-mouth the Democratic ones.

And exploit all the veterans and all the still-serving personnel in a cheap and tawdry political trick to try to bury the truth: that John Kerry said the president had been stupid.

And to continue this slander as late as this morning, as biased or gullible or lazy newscasters nodded in sleepwalking assent.

71

Senator McCain became a front man in a collective lie to break sticks over the heads of Democrats—one of them his friend, another his fellow veteran, legless, for whom he should weep and applaud, or at minimum about whom he should stay quiet.

That was beneath the senator from Arizona.

And it was all because of an imaginary insult to the troops that his party cynically manufactured out of a desperation and a futility as deep as that of Congressman Brooks when he went hunting for Senator Sumner.

This is our beloved country now as you have redefined it, Mr. Bush.

Get a tortured Vietnam veteran to attack a decorated Vietnam veteran in defense of military personnel whom that decorated veteran did not insult.

Or get your henchmen to take advantage of the evil lingering dregs of the fear of miscegenation in Tennessee, in your party's advertisements against Harold Ford.

Or get the satellites who orbit around you, like Rush Limbaugh, to exploit the illness—and the bipartisanship—of Michael J. Fox. Yes, get someone to make fun of the cripple.

Oh, and sir, don't forget to drag your own wife into it.

"It's always easy," she said of Mr. Fox's commercials—and she used this phrase twice—"to manipulate people's feelings."

Where on earth might the First Lady have gotten that idea, Mr. President?

From your endless manipulation of people's feelings about terrorism?

"However they put it," you said Monday of the Democrats, on the subject of Iraq, "their approach comes down to this: The terrorists win, and America loses."

No manipulation of feelings there. No manipulation of the charlatans of your administration into the only truth-tellers.

No shocked outrage at the Kerry insult that wasn't; no subtle smile as the First Lady silently sticks the knife in Michael J. Fox's back; no attempt on the campaign trail to bury the reality that you have already assured that the terrorists are winning.

Winning in Iraq, sir.

Winning in America, sir.

There we have chaos—joint U.S.-Iraqi checkpoints at Sadr City, the base of the radical Shiite militias, and the Americans have been ordered out by the prime minister of Iraq—and our secretary of defense doesn't even know about it!

And here we have deliberate, systematic, institutionalized lying and smearing and terrorizing—a code of deceit that somehow permits a president to say, "If you listen carefully for a Democrat plan for success, they don't have one."

Permits him to say this while his plan in Iraq has amounted to a twisted version of the advice once offered to Lyndon Johnson about his Iraq, called Vietnam:

Instead of "Declare victory and get out," we now have "Declare victory and stay indefinitely."

And also here—we have institutionalized the terrorizing of the opposition.

True domestic terror:

Critics of your administration in the media receive letters filled with fake anthrax.

Braying newspapers applaud or laugh or reveal details the FBI wished kept quiet, and thus impede or ruin the investigation.

A series of reactionary columnists encourages treason charges against a newspaper that published "national security information" that was openly available on the Internet.

One radio critic receives a letter threatening the revelation of as much personal information about her as can be obtained and expressing the hope that someone will then shoot her with an AK-47 machine gun.

And finally, a critic of an incumbent Republican senator, a critic armed with nothing but words, is attacked by the senator's supporters and thrown to the floor in full view of television cameras as if someone really did want to reenact the intent—and the rage—of the day Preston Brooks found Senator Charles Sumner.

Of course, Mr. President, *you* did none of these things.

You instructed no one to mail the fake anthrax, nor undermine the FBI's case, nor call for the execution of the editors of *The New York Times,* nor threaten to assassinate Stephanie Miller, nor beat up a man yelling at Senator George Allen, nor have the First Lady knife Michael J. Fox, nor tell John McCain to lie about John Kerry.

No, you did not.

And the genius of the thing is the same as in King Henry's rhetorical question about Archbishop Thomas Becket: "Who will rid me of this meddlesome priest?"

All you have to do, sir, is hand out enough new canes.

11

Where Are the Checks and Balances?

November 6, 2006

The date will indicate that this one was delivered the night before the 2006 election. It was a final attempt to remind voters why this particular vote was so important, and to counter the Republicans' efforts to use Saddam Hussein's trial and John Kerry's joke to bring out its base. This was the only Comment over which anybody in management at NBC or MSNBC voiced any concern about any part of what I intended to say. The original version ended: "Making it up, as you went along, unchecked and unbalanced. *And that must change. Tomorrow.* Vote." MSNBC's general manager, Dan Abrams, astutely observed that I would be reading this particular piece from the very same stage from which I would be coanchoring our coverage of the following night's election, and it was probably a full foot over the foul line to have explicitly told people how they should vote. Besides, as we all realized, if they hadn't figured out my point of view by that point in the piece, or that point in the campaign, my telling them now wasn't going to make any difference to them, or to the country.

———

WE ARE, as every generation, inseparable from our own time.

Thus is our perspective inevitably that of the explorer looking into the wrong end of the telescope.

But even accounting for our myopia, it's hard to imagine there have been many elections more important than this one, certainly not in non-presidential years.

And so we look at the verdict in the trial of Saddam Hussein yesterday, and with the very phrase "October (or November) Surprise" now a part of our vernacular, and the chest-thumping coming from so many of the Republican campaigners today, each of us must wonder about the convenience of the timing of his conviction and sentencing.

But let us give history and coincidence the benefit of the doubt—let's say it's just "happened" that way—and for a moment not look into the wrong end of the telescope.

Let's perceive instead the bigger picture:

Saddam Hussein, found guilty in an Iraqi court. Who can argue against that? He is officially what the world always knew he was: a war criminal.

Mr. Bush, was this imprimatur worth the cost of 2,832 American lives, and thousands more American lives yet to be lost?

Is the conviction of Saddam Hussein the reason you went to war in Iraq?

Or did you go to war in Iraq because of the weapons of mass destruction that did not exist?

Or did you go to war in Iraq because of the connection between Iraq and al-Qaeda that did not exist?

Or did you go to war in Iraq to break the bonds of tyranny there, while installing the mechanisms of tyranny here?

Or did you go to war in Iraq because you felt the need to wreak vengeance against somebody, anybody?

Or did you go to war in Iraq to contain a rogue state which, months earlier, your own administration had declared had been fully contained by sanctions?

Or did you go to war in Iraq to keep gas prices down?

How startling it was, sir, to hear you introduce oil to your stump speeches over the weekend.

Not four years removed from the most dismissive, the most condescending, the most ridiculing denials of the very hint at, as Mr. Rumsfeld put it, this "nonsense," there you were, campaigning in Colorado, in Nebraska, in Florida, in Kansas—suddenly turning this "unpatriotic idea" into a platform plank.

"You can imagine a world in which these extremists and radicals got control of energy resources," you told us. "And then you can imagine them saying, 'We're going to pull a bunch of oil off the market to run your price of oil up unless you do the following.'"

Having frightened us, having bullied us, having lied to us, having ignored and rewritten the Constitution under our noses, having stayed the course, having denied you've stayed the course, having belittled us about "timelines" but instead extolled "benchmarks," you've now resorted, sir, to this?

We must stay in Iraq to save the two-dollar gallon of gas?

Mr. President, there is no other conclusion we can draw as we go to the polls tomorrow:

Sir, you have been making this up as you went along.

This country was founded to prevent anybody from making it up as they went along.

Those vaunted Founding Fathers of ours have been so quoted up that they appear as marble statues, like the chiseled guards of China, or the faces on Mount Rushmore. But in fact they were practical people, and the thing they obviously feared most was a government of men and not laws.

They provided the checks and balances for a reason.

No one man could run the government the way he saw fit—unless he, at the least, took into consideration what those he governed saw.

A House of Representatives would be the people's eyes.

A Senate would be the corrective force on that House.

An executive would do the work, and hold the Constitution to his chest like his child.

A Supreme Court would oversee it all.

Checks and balances.

Where did that go, Mr. Bush? And what price did we pay because we have let it go?

Saddam Hussein will get out of Iraq the same way 2,832 Americans have and thousands more. He'll get out faster than we will. And if nothing changes tomorrow, you, sir, will be out of the White House long before the rest of us can say we are out of Iraq.

And whose fault is this?

Not truly yours. You took advantage of those of us who were afraid, and those of us who believed unity and nation took precedence over all else.

But we let you take that advantage. And so we let you go to war in Iraq to oust Saddam or find nonexistent weapons or avenge 9/11 or fight terrorists who only got there after we did or as cover to change the fabric of our Constitution or for lower prices at the Texaco or . . . ?

There are still a few hours left before the polls open, sir. There are many rationalizations still untried.

And whatever your motives of the moment, we the people have, in true good faith and with the genuine patriotism of self-sacrifice (of which you have shown you know nothing), we have let you go on making it up as you went along.

Unchecked and unbalanced.

Vote.

12

Lessons from the Vietnam War

November 20, 2006

President Bush went to Vietnam in November 2006 to attend the Asia-Pacific Economic Cooperation meeting. Hours before his trip, the White House website trumpeted the president's tour and posted the flag of Vietnam—*South* Vietnam—the one last used in 1975. How appropriate, given this administration's tortured relationship with, and blissful lack of concern for, both history and reality! Worse was yet to come when Mr. Bush took questions and showed that his understanding of the meaning of our tragedy in Southeast Asia was not even a fraction of a percentage greater than his website's awareness of which banners—and countries—had vanished three decades before.

IT IS A SHAME and it is embarrassing to us all when President Bush travels eight thousand miles only to wind up avoiding reality again.

And it is pathetic to listen to a man talk unrealistically about Vietnam who permitted the "Swift-Boating" of not one but two American heroes of that war in consecutive presidential campaigns.

But most importantly—important beyond measure—his avoidance of reality is going to wind up killing more Americans.

And that is indefensible and fatal.

Asked if there were lessons about Iraq to be found in our experience in Vietnam, Mr. Bush said that there were, and he immediately proved he had no clue what they were.

"One lesson is," he said, "that we tend to want there to be instant success in the world, and the task in Iraq is going to take a while."

"We'll succeed," the president concluded, "unless we quit."

If that's the lesson about Iraq that Mr. Bush sees in Vietnam, then he needs a tutor.

Or we need somebody else making the decisions about Iraq.

Mr. Bush, there are a dozen central, essential lessons to be derived from our nightmare in Vietnam, but "We'll succeed unless we quit" is not one of them.

The primary one—which should be as obvious to you as the latest opinion poll showing that only 31 percent of this country agrees with your tragic Iraq policy—is that if you try to pursue a war for which the nation has lost its stomach, you and it are finished. Ask Lyndon Johnson.

The second most important lesson of Vietnam, Mr. Bush: If you don't have a stable local government to work with, you can keep sending in Americans until hell freezes over and it will not matter. Ask Vietnamese presidents Diem or Thieu.

The third vital lesson of Vietnam, Mr. Bush: Don't pretend it's something it's not. For decades we were warned that if we didn't stop "communist aggression" in Vietnam, communist agitators would infiltrate and devour the small nations of the world and make their insidious way stealthily to our doorstep. The war machine of 1968 had this "domino theory." Your war machine of 2006 has this nonsense about Iraq as "the central front in the war on terror."

The fourth pivotal lesson of Vietnam, Mr. Bush: If the same idiots who told Lyndon Johnson and Richard Nixon to stay there for the sake of "peace with honor" are now telling you to stay in Iraq, they're probably just as wrong now as they were then—Dr. Kissinger.

And the fifth crucial lesson of Vietnam, Mr. Bush—which somebody should've told you about long before you plunged this country into Iraq—is that if you lie your country into a war—your war—your presidency will be consigned to the scrap heap of history.

Consider your fellow Texan, sir. After Kennedy's assassination, Lyndon Johnson held the country together after a national tragedy, not unlike you did. He had lofty goals and tried to reshape society for the better. And he is remembered for Vietnam, and for the lies he and his government told to get us there and keep us there, and for the Americans who needlessly died there.

As you will be remembered for Iraq, and for the lies you and your government told to get us there and keep us there, and for the Americans who have needlessly died there and who will needlessly die there tomorrow.

This president has his fictitious Iraqi WMD, and his lies—disguised as subtle hints—linking Saddam Hussein to 9/11, and his reason of the week for keeping us there when all the evidence for at least three years has told us we need to get as many of our kids out as quickly as possible.

That president had his fictitious attacks on Navy ships in the Gulf of Tonkin in 1964, and the next thing any of us knew, the Senate had voted 88–2 to approve the blank check with which Lyndon Johnson paid for our trip into hell.

And yet President Bush just saw the grim reminders of that trip into hell: the fifty-eight thousand Americans and millions of Vietnamese killed; the ten thousand civilians who've been blown up by land mines since we pulled out; the genocide in the neighboring country of Cambodia, which we triggered. Yet these parallels—and these lessons—eluded President Bush entirely.

And in particular, the one overarching lesson about Iraq that should've been written everywhere he looked in Vietnam went unseen.

"We'll succeed unless we quit"?

Mr. Bush, we *did* quit in Vietnam!

A decade later than we should have, fifty-eight thousand dead later than we should have, but we finally came to our senses. The stable, burgeoning, vivid country you just saw there, is there because we finally had the good sense to declare victory and get out!

The domino theory was nonsense, sir. Our departure from Vietnam emboldened no one. Communism did not spread like a contagion around the world.

And most importantly—as President Reagan's assistant secretary of state, Lawrence Korb, said on this newscast Friday—we were only in a position to win the Cold War because we quit in Vietnam.

We went home. And instead it was the Russians who learned nothing from Vietnam, and who repeated every one of our mistakes when they went into Afghanistan. And alienated their own people, and killed their own children, and bankrupted their own economy, and allowed us to win the Cold War.

We awakened so late, but we did awaken.

Finally, in Vietnam, we learned the lesson. We stopped endlessly squandering lives and treasure and the focus of a nation on an impossible and irrelevant dream. But you are still doing exactly that, tonight, in Iraq. And these lessons from Vietnam, Mr. Bush, these priceless, transparent lessons, writ large as if across the very sky, are still a mystery to you.

"We'll succeed unless we quit."

No, sir.

We will succeed against terrorism, for our country's needs, toward binding up the nation's wounds, when *you* quit—quit the monumental lie that is our presence in Iraq.

And in the interim, Mr. Bush, an American kid will be killed there, probably tonight or tomorrow.

And here, sir, endeth the lesson.

13

Free Speech, Failed Speakers, and the Delusion of Grandeur

November 30, 2006

Why anyone would invite Newt Gingrich to speak about anything is a mystery to me. He barely made sense in Congress. His "Contract with America" was less equitable than those offered by mobile phone service providers. His stance during the Clinton impeachment was hypocritical to the point of hilarity. And his subsequent commentary for Fox Noise Channel (sorry, Fixed News Channel) has bordered on the delirious. Plus, there is the unavoidable symbolism provided by the reality that he answers to the name "Newt."

Gingrich's remarks that prompted this comment might have been his first attempt to fire up his base for a possible presidential run, or it might have been something more ominous. At the annual Nackey S. Loeb First Amendment Award Dinner in Manchester, New Hampshire, on November 27, 2006, the former Speaker of the House argued that in order to save ourselves from terrorists we would have to curtail one of our most sacred constitutional rights: freedom of speech. My immediate response to this was, well, "Gingrich is a clown and a hypocrite, and nobody takes him seriously anyway." But viewed in the context of the Republicans' larger War on American Values (remember habeas corpus?), the speech was frightening. Earlier in the week I had asked George Washington University Law School constitutional scholar Jonathan Turley whether Gingrich's plan could ever gain traction. His response, I think, put it quite eloquently:

> *You know, this really could happen. I mean, the fact is that the First Amendment is an abstraction, and when you put up against it the idea of incinerating millions of people, there will be millions of citizens that respond like some Pavlovian response and deliver up rights. We've already seen that. People don't seem to appreciate that you really can't save a constitution by destroying it.*

HERE, AS PROMISED, a Special Comment about free speech, failed Speakers, and the delusion of grandeur.

"This is a serious long-term war," the man at the podium cried, "and it will inevitably lead us to want to know what is said in every suspect place in the country."

Some in the audience must have thought they were hearing an arsonist give the keynote address at a convention of firefighters.

This was the annual Loeb First Amendment Dinner in Manchester, New Hampshire—a public cherishing of freedom of speech—in the state with the two-fisted motto "Live Free or Die." And the arsonist at the microphone, the former Speaker of the House, Newt Gingrich, was insisting that we must attach an "on-off button" to free speech.

He offered the time-tested excuse trotted out by our demagogues since even before the republic was founded: widespread death, of Americans, in America, possibly at the hands of Americans. But updated, now, to include terrorists using the Internet for recruitment. End result: "losing a city."

The colonial English defended their repression with words like these.

And so did the slave states.

And so did the policemen who shot strikers.

And so did Lindbergh's America First crowd, and so did those who interned Japanese Americans, and so did those behind the Red Scare, and so did Nixon's plumbers.

The genuine proportion of the threat is always irrelevant. The fear the threat is exploited to create becomes the only reality.

"We will adopt rules of engagement that use every technology we can find," Mr. Gingrich continued about terrorists—formerly communists, formerly hippies, formerly fifth columnists, formerly anarchists, formerly redcoats—"to break up their capacity to use the Internet, to break up their capacity to use free speech."

Mr. Gingrich, the British "broke up our capacity to use free speech" in the 1770s. The pro-slavery leaders "broke up our capacity to use free speech" in the 1850s. The FBI and CIA "broke up our capacity to use free speech" in the 1960s.

It is in those groups where you would have found your kindred spirits, Mr. Gingrich.

Those who had no faith in freedom, no faith in this country, and ultimately no faith even in the strength of their own ideas to stand up on their own legs without having the playing field tilted entirely to their benefit.

"It will lead us to learn," Gingrich continued, "how to close down every website that is dangerous, and it will lead us to a very severe approach to people who advocate the killing of Americans and advocate the use of nuclear and biological weapons."

That we have always had "a very severe approach" to these people is insufficient for Mr. Gingrich's ends.

He wants to somehow ban the *idea*. Even though everyone who has ever protested a movie or a piece of music or a book has learned the same lesson:

Try to suppress it, and you only validate it.

Make it illegal, and you make it the subject of curiosity.

Say it cannot be said, and it will instead be screamed.

And on top of the thundering danger in his eagerness to sell out free-dom of speech, there is a sadder sound still—the tinny crash of a garbage can lid on a sidewalk.

Whatever dreams of Internet censorship float like a miasma in Mr. Gingrich's personal swamp, whatever hopes he has of an Iron Firewall, the simple fact is, technically they won't work.

As of tomorrow they will have been defeated by a free computer download.

Mere hours after Gingrich's speech in New Hampshire, the University of Toronto announced it had come up with a program called "psiphon" to liberate those in countries in which the Internet is regu-lated. Places like China and Iran, where political ideas are so barren, and political leaders so desperate, that they put up computer firewalls to keep thought and freedom out.

The psiphon device is a relay of sorts that can surreptitiously link a computer user in an imprisoned country to another in a free one. The Chinese think the wall works, yet the ideas—good ideas, bad ideas, in-different ideas—pass through anyway.

The same way the Soviet bloc was defeated by the images of Western material bounty.

If your hopes of thought control can be defeated, Mr. Gingrich, merely by one computer whiz staying up an extra half hour and devising a new "firewall hop," what is all this apocalyptic hyperbole for?

"I further think," you said in Manchester, "we should propose a Geneva Convention for fighting terrorism, which makes very clear that those who would fight outside the rules of law, those who would use weapons of mass destruction, and those who would target civilians are in fact subject to a totally different set of rules, that allow us to protect civ-ilization by defeating barbarism."

Well, Mr. Gingrich, what is more "massively destructive" than trying to get us to give you our freedom?

And what is someone seeking to hamstring the First Amendment doing, if not "fighting outside the rules of law"?

And what is the suppression of knowledge and freedom, if not "barbarism"?

The explanation, of course, is in one last quote from Mr. Gingrich from New Hampshire and another from last week:

"I want to suggest to you," he said about these Internet restrictions, "that we right now should be impaneling people to look seriously at a level of supervision that we would never dream of if it weren't for the scale of the threat."

And who should those "impaneled" people be?

Funny I should ask, isn't it, Mr. Gingrich?

"I am not 'running' for president," you told a reporter from *Fortune* magazine. "I am seeking to create a movement to win the future by offering a series of solutions so compelling that if the American people say I have to be president, it will happen."

Newt Gingrich sees in terrorism, not something to be exterminated, but something to be exploited.

It's his golden opportunity, isn't it?

"Rallying a nation," you might say, "to hysteria, to sweep us up into the White House with powers that will make martial law seem like anarchy."

That's from the original version of the movie *The Manchurian Candidate*—the chilling words of Angela Lansbury's character as she first promises to sell her country to the Chinese and Russians, then reveals she'll double-cross them and keep all the power herself, waving the flag every time she subjugates another freedom.

Within the frame of our experience as a free and freely argumentative people, it is almost impossible to conceive that there are those among us who might approach the kind of animal wildness of fiction like that—those who would willingly transform our beloved country into something false and terrible.

Who among us can look to our own histories, or those of our ancestors who struggled to get here, or who struggled to get freedom after they were forced here, and not tear up when we read Frederick Douglass's words from a century and a half ago: "Freedom must take the day."

And who among us can look to our collective history and not see its turning points—like the Civil War, like Watergate, like the Revolution itself—in which the right idea defeated the wrong idea on the battlefield that is the marketplace of ideas?

But apparently there are some of us who cannot see that the only future for America is one that cherishes the freedoms won in the past, one in which we vanquish bad ideas with better ones, and in which we fight for liberty by having more liberty, not less.

"I am seeking to create a movement to win the future by offering a series of solutions so compelling that if the American people say I have to be president, it will happen."

What a dark place your world must be, Mr. Gingrich, where the way to save America is to destroy America. I will awaken every day of my life thankful I am not with you in that dark place.

And I will awaken every day of my life thankful that you are entitled to tell me about it. And that you are entitled to show me what an evil idea it represents, and what a cynical mind. And that you are entitled to do all that, thanks to the very freedoms you seek to suffocate.

14

On Sacrifice

January 2, 2007

At the beginning of 2007 we began to hear of President Bush's impending "new strategy" for the war in Iraq, what came to be known as "the Surge." The president would give a speech on January 10 outlining the strategy, and as usual his speechwriters made sure to link any opposition to the president's plans to a lack of appreciation for the sacrifices made by the troops: "They have watched their comrades give their lives to ensure our liberty. We mourn the loss of every fallen American—and we owe it to them to build a future worthy of their sacrifice." Of course, in order to do that, you actually need a plan that has a prayer of working. Short of that, you are simply and starkly killing our brothers and sisters, and sons and daughters, and friends and neighbors, to justify having killed the ones you killed earlier.

IF IN YOUR PRESENCE an individual tried to sacrifice an American serviceman or -woman, would you intervene?

Would you at least protest?

What if he had already sacrificed 3,003 of them?

What if he had already sacrificed 3,003 of them and was then to announce his intention to sacrifice hundreds, maybe thousands, more?

This is where we stand tonight with the BBC report of President Bush's "new Iraq strategy" and his impending speech to the nation, which, according to a quoted senior American official, will be about troop increases and "sacrifice."

The president has delayed, dawdled, and deferred for the month since the release of the Iraq Study Group report.

He has seemingly heard out everybody, and listened to none of them.

If the BBC is right—and we can only pray it is not—he has settled on the only solution all the true experts agree cannot possibly work: more American personnel in Iraq, not as trainers for Iraqi troops, but as part of some flabby plan for "sacrifice."

"Sacrifice"!

More American servicemen and -women will have their lives risked.

More American servicemen and -women will have their lives ended.

More American families will have to bear the unbearable and rationalize the unforgivable—"sacrifice"—sacrifice now, sacrifice tomorrow, sacrifice forever.

And more Americans—more even than the two-thirds who already believe we need fewer troops in Iraq, not more—will have to conclude the president does not have any idea what he's doing, and that other Americans will have to die for that reason.

It must now be branded as propaganda—for even the president cannot truly feel that very many people still believe him to be competent in this area, let alone "The Decider."

But from our impeccable reporter at the Pentagon, Jim Miklaszewski, tonight comes confirmation of something called "surge and accelerate"—as many as twenty thousand additional troops—for "political purposes."

This in line with what we had previously heard, that this will be proclaimed a short-term measure, for the stated purpose of increasing security in and around Baghdad and giving an Iraqi government a chance to establish some kind of order.

This is palpable nonsense, Mr. Bush.

If this is your intention—if the centerpiece of your announcement next week will be "sacrifice"—sacrifice your intention, not more American lives!

As Senator Joseph Biden has pointed out, the new troops might improve the ratio our forces face relative to those living in Baghdad (friend and foe), from 200 to 1 to just 100 to 1.

"Sacrifice"?

No. A drop in the bucket.

The additional men and women you have sentenced to go there, sir, will serve only as targets.

They will not be there "short-term," Mr. Bush; for many it will mean a year or more in death's shadow.

This is not temporary, Mr. Bush. For the Americans who will die because of you, it will be as permanent as it gets.

The various rationales for what Mr. Bush will reportedly rechristen "sacrifice" constitute a very thin gruel indeed.

The former labor secretary Robert Reich says Senator John McCain told him that the "surge" would help the "morale" of the troops already in Iraq.

If Mr. McCain truly said that, and truly believes it, he has either forgotten completely his own experience in Vietnam, or he is unaware of the recent *Military Times* poll indicating only 38 percent of our active military want to see more troops sent—or Mr. McCain has departed from reality.

Then there is the argument that to take any steps toward reducing troop numbers would show weakness to the enemy in Iraq, or to the terrorists around the world.

This simplistic logic ignores the inescapable fact that we have indeed already showed weakness to the enemy, and to the terrorists.

We have shown them that we will let our own people be killed for no good reason. We have now shown them that we will continue to do so.

We have shown them our stupidity.

Mr. Bush, your judgment about Iraq—and now about "sacrifice"—is at variance with your people's, to the point of delusion.

Your most respected generals see no value in a "surge"—they could not possibly see it in this madness of "sacrifice."

The Iraq Study Group told you it would be a mistake. Perhaps dozens more have told you it would be a mistake. And you threw their wisdom back until you finally heard what you wanted to hear, like some child drawing straws and then saying "best two out of three . . . best three out of five . . . hundredth one counts."

Your citizens, the people for whom you work, have told you they do not want this, and moreover, they do not want you to do this. Yet once again, sir, you have ignored all of us.

Mr. Bush, you do not own this country!

To those Republicans who have not broken free from the slavery of partisanship—those bonded still to this president and this administration, and now bonded to this "sacrifice"—proceed at your own peril.

John McCain may still hear the applause of small crowds—he has somehow inured himself to the hypocrisy, and the tragedy, of a man who considers himself the ultimate realist, courting the votes of those who support the government telling visitors to the Grand Canyon that it was caused by the Great Flood. That Mr. McCain is selling himself off to the irrational right, parcel by parcel, like some great landowner facing bankruptcy, seems to be obvious to everybody but himself.

Or maybe it is obvious to him and he simply no longer cares.

But to the rest of you in the Republican Party:

We need you to speak up, right now, in defense of your country's most precious assets—the lives of its citizens who are in harm's way. If you do not, you are not serving this nation's interests—nor your own.

November should have told you this.

The opening of the new Congress on Wednesday and Thursday should tell you this.

Next time, those missing Republicans will be you.

And to the Democrats now yoked to the helm of this sinking ship, you proceed at your own peril as well.

President Bush may not be very good at reality, but he and Mr. Cheney and Mr. Rove are still gifted at letting American troops be killed and then turning their deaths to their own political advantage.

The equation is simple: This country does not want more troops in Iraq. It wants fewer. Go and make it happen, or go and look for other work.

Yet you Democrats must assume that even if you take the most obvious of courses, and cut off funding for the war, Mr. Bush will ignore you as long as possible, or will find the money elsewhere, or will spend the money meant to protect the troops and repurpose it to keep as many troops there as long as he can keep them there.

Because that's what this is all about, is it not, Mr. Bush? That is what this "sacrifice" has been for. To continue this senseless, endless war.

You have dressed it up in the clothing, first of a hunt for weapons of mass destruction—then of liberation—then of regional imperative—then of oil prices—and now in these new terms of "sacrifice." It's like a damned game of Colorforms, isn't it, sir? This senseless, endless war.

But it has not been senseless in two ways.

It has succeeded, Mr. Bush, in enabling you to deaden the collective mind of this country to the pointlessness of endless war, against the wrong people, in the wrong place, at the wrong time.

It has gotten many of us used to the idea—the virtual "white noise"—of conflict far away, of the deaths of young Americans, of vague "sacrifice" for some fluid cause, too complicated to be interpreted except in terms of the very important-sounding but ultimately meaningless phrase "the war on terror."

And the war's second accomplishment—your second accomplishment, sir—is to have taken money out of the pockets of every American, even out of the pockets of the dead soldiers on the battlefield, and their families, and to have given that money to the war profiteers.

Because if you sell the Army a thousand Humvees, you can't sell them any more until the first thousand have been destroyed.

The servicemen and -women are ancillary to the equation.

This is about the planned obsolescence of ordnance, isn't it, Mr. Bush? And the building of detention centers? And the design of a $125-million courtroom complex at Gitmo, complete with restaurants?

At least the war profiteers have made their money, sir.

And we here highly resolve that these dead shall not have died in vain.

You have insisted, Mr. Bush, that we must not lose in Iraq, that if we don't fight them there, we will fight them here—as if the corollary were somehow true, that by fighting them there we will not have to fight them here.

And yet you have remade our country, and not remade it for the better, on the premise that we need to be ready to "fight them here" anyway and always.

In point of fact, even if the civil war in Iraq somehow ended tomorrow, and the risk to Americans there ended with it, we would have already suffered a defeat—not fatal, not world-changing, not, but for the lives lost, of enduring consequence.

But this country has already lost in Iraq, sir.

Your policy in Iraq has already had its crushing impact on our safety here.

You have already fomented new terrorism and new terrorists.

You have already stoked paranoia.

You have already pitted Americans one against the other.

We will have to live with it.

We will have to live with what—of the fabric of our nation—you have already "sacrificed."

The only object still admissible in this debate is the quickest and safest exit for our people there.

But you—and soon, Mr. Bush, it will be you and you alone—still insist otherwise.

And our sons and daughters and fathers and mothers will be sacrificed there tonight, sir, so that you can say you did not "lose in Iraq."

Our policy in Iraq has been criticized for being indescribable, for being inscrutable, for being ineffable. But it is all too easily understood now.

First we sent Americans to their deaths for your lie, Mr. Bush.

Now we are sending them to their deaths for your ego.

If what is reported is true—if your decision is made and the "sacrifice" is ordered—take a page instead from the man at whose funeral you so eloquently spoke this morning—Gerald Ford.

Put pragmatism and the healing of a nation ahead of some kind of misguided vision.

Atone.

"Sacrifice," Mr. Bush?

No, sir, this is not "sacrifice." This has now become "human sacrifice." And it must stop. And you can stop it.

Next week, make us all look wrong.

Our meaningless sacrifice in Iraq must stop. And you must stop it.

15

Bush's Legacy: The President Who Cried Wolf

January 11, 2007

At a time when an unquestionable majority of Americans already believed that invading Iraq had been a horrific mistake, that the war itself
was going very badly, and that President Bush did not have a clear
plan for handling that conflict, Mr. Bush announced his intention to
escalate our involvement and extend it indefinitely, a move meant to
reassure a war-weary nation that he had everything under control.
Bush's speech on January 10 was all that was promised and more. He
would pay no attention to the Iraq Study Group, or to the relatively few
wise voices in his party, nor to anyone in the military who disagreed
with him, nor to the roughly 83 percent of Americans who did not want
a troop increase, nor—as usual—to anyone who disagreed with him.

ONLY THIS PRESIDENT, only in this time, only with this dangerous, even
messianic certitude, could answer a country demanding an exit strategy
from Iraq by offering an entrance strategy for Iran.

Only this president could look out over a vista of 3,008 dead and 22,834 wounded in Iraq, and finally say, "Where mistakes have been made, the responsibility rests with me"—only to follow that by proposing to repeat the identical mistake—in Iran.

Only this president could extol the "thoughtful recommendations of the Iraq Study Group," and then take its most farsighted recommendation—"engage Syria and Iran"—and transform it into "threaten Syria and Iran," when al-Qaeda would like nothing better than for us to threaten Syria, and when Iranian president Mahmoud Ahmadinejad would like nothing better than to be threatened by us.

This is diplomacy by skimming; it is internationalism by drawing pictures of Superman in the margins of the textbooks; it is a presidency of CliffsNotes.

And to Iran and Syria—and, yes, also to the insurgents in Iraq—we must look like a country run by the equivalent of the drunken pest who gets battered to the floor of the saloon by one punch, then staggers to his feet and shouts at the other guy's friends, "Okay, which one of you is next?"

Mr. Bush, the question is no longer "What are you thinking?" but rather "Are you thinking at all?"

"I have made it clear to the prime minister and Iraq's other leaders that America's commitment is not open-ended," you said last night.

And yet—without any authorization from the public, which spoke so loudly and clearly to you in November's elections—without any consultation with a Congress in which key members of your own party, including Senators Sam Brownback, Norm Coleman, and Chuck Hagel, are fleeing for higher ground—without any awareness that you are doing exactly the opposite of what Baker-Hamilton urged you to do—you seem to be ready to make an open-ended commitment (on America's behalf) to do whatever you want, in Iran.

Our military, Mr. Bush, is already stretched so thin by this bogus adventure in Iraq that even a majority of serving personnel are willing to tell pollsters that they are dissatisfied with your prosecution of the war.

It is so weary that many of the troops you have just consigned to Iraq will be on their second tours or their third tours or their fourth tours—and now you're going to make them take on Iran and Syria as well?

Who is left to go and fight, sir?

Who are you going to send to "interrupt the flow of support from Iran and Syria"? Laura and Barney?

The line is from the movie *Chinatown,* and I quote it often: "Middle of a drought," the mortician chuckles, "and the water commissioner drowns. Only in L.A.!"

Middle of a debate over the lives and deaths of another 21,500 of our citizens in Iraq, and the president wants to saddle up against Iran and Syria.

Maybe that's the point—to shift the attention away from just how absurd and childish this latest war strategy is—strategy, that is, for the war already under way, and not the one on deck.

We are going to put 17,500 more troops into Baghdad and 4,000 more into Anbar Province to give the Iraqi government "breathing space." In and of itself that is an awful and insulting term. The lives of 21,500 more Americans endangered, to give "breathing space" to a government that just turned the first and perhaps the most sober act of any democracy—the capital punishment of an ousted dictator—into a vengeance lynching so barbaric and so lacking in the solemnities necessary for credible authority that it might have offended the Ku Klux Klan of the nineteenth century.

And what will our men and women in Iraq do? The ones who will truly live—and die—during what Mr. Bush said last night will be a "year ahead" that "will demand more patience, sacrifice, and resolve"?

They will try to seal Sadr City and other parts of Baghdad where the civil war is worst.

Mr. Bush did not mention that while our people are trying to do that, the factions in the civil war will no longer have to focus on killing each other, but rather they can focus anew on killing our people.

Because last night the president foolishly all but announced that we will be sending these 21,500 poor souls, but no more after that, and if the whole thing fizzles out, we're going home.

The plan fails militarily.

The plan fails symbolically.

The plan fails politically.

Most importantly, perhaps, Mr. Bush, the plan fails because it still depends on your credibility.

You speak of mistakes and of the responsibility "resting" with you. But you do not admit to making those mistakes. And you offer us nothing to justify this clenched fist toward Iran and Syria.

In fact, when you briefed news correspondents off the record before the speech, they were told, once again, "If you knew what we knew . . . if you saw what we saw . . ."

"If you knew what we knew" was how we got into this morass in Iraq in the first place.

The problem arose when it turned out that the question wasn't whether we knew what you knew, but whether *you* knew what you knew.

You, sir, have become the president who cried wolf.

All that you say about Iraq now could be gospel. All that you say about Iran and Syria now could be prescient and essential.

We no longer have a clue, sir. We have heard too many stories.

Many of us are as inclined to believe you just shuffled the director of national intelligence over to the State Department because he thought you were wrong about Iran.

Many of us are as inclined to believe you just put a pilot in charge of ground wars in Iraq and Afghanistan because he would be truly useful in an air war next door in Iran.

Your assurances, sir, and your demands that we trust you, have lost all shape and texture. They are now merely fertilizer for conspiracy theories.

They are now fertilizer, indeed. The pile has been built slowly and with seeming care.

I read this list last night, before the president's speech, and it bears repeating because its shape and texture are perceptible only in such a context:

Before Mr. Bush was elected, he said nation-building was wrong for America.

Now he says it is vital.

He said he would never put U.S. troops under foreign control.

Last night he promised to embed them in Iraqi units.

He told us about WMD.

Mobile labs.

Secret sources.

Aluminum tubes.

Yellowcake.

He has told us the war is necessary:

Because Saddam was a material threat.

Because of 9/11.

Because of Osama bin Laden. Al-Qaeda. Terrorism in general.

To liberate Iraq. To spread freedom. To spread democracy. To prevent terrorism by gas price increases.

Because this was a guy who tried to kill his dad.

Because—439 words into the speech last night—he trotted out 9/11 again.

In advocating and prosecuting this war he passed on a chance to get Abu Musab al-Zarqawi.

To get Muqtada al-Sadr. To get bin Laden.

He sent in fewer troops than the generals told him to. He ordered the Iraqi army disbanded and the Iraqi government "de-Baathified."

He shortchanged Iraqi training. He neglected to plan for widespread looting. He did not anticipate sectarian violence.

He sent in troops without lifesaving equipment. He gave jobs to foreign contractors and not Iraqis. He staffed U.S. positions there based on partisanship, not professionalism.

He and his government told us America had prevailed, mission accomplished, the resistance was in its last throes.

He has insisted more troops were not necessary. He has now insisted more troops are necessary.

He has insisted it's up to the generals, and then removed some of the generals who said more troops would not be necessary.

He has trumpeted the turning points:

The fall of Baghdad, the death of Uday and Qusay, the capture of Saddam. A provisional government, a charter, a constitution, the trial of Saddam. Elections, purple fingers, another government, the death of Saddam.

He has assured us we would be greeted as liberators—with flowers.

As they stood up, we would stand down. We would stay the course; we were never about "stay the course."

We would never have to go door to door in Baghdad. And, last night, that to gain Iraqis' trust, we would go door to door in Baghdad.

He told us the enemy was al-Qaeda, foreign fighters, terrorists, Baathists, and now Iran and Syria.

He told us the war would pay for itself. It would cost $1.7 billion. $100 billion. $400 billion. Half a trillion. Last night's speech alone cost another $6 billion.

And after all of that, now it is his credibility versus that of generals, diplomats, allies, Democrats, Republicans, the Iraq Study Group, past presidents, voters last November, and the majority of the American people.

Oh, and one more to add, tonight: Oceania has always been at war with East Asia.

Mr. Bush, this is madness.

You have lost the military. You have lost the Congress to the Democrats. You have lost most of the Iraqis. You have lost many of the Republicans. You have lost our allies.

You are losing the credibility, not just of your presidency, but more importantly, of the office itself.

And most imperatively, you are guaranteeing that more American troops will be losing their lives, and more families their loved ones. You are guaranteeing it!

This becomes your legacy, sir: how many of those you addressed last night as your "fellow citizens" you just sent to their deaths.

And for what, Mr. Bush?

So the next president has to pull the survivors out of Iraq instead of you?

16

Bush Shoots for *Jaws,*
Delivers *Jaws 2*

January 30, 2007

This Special Comment came in response to President Bush's State of the Union speech of January 23, 2007, and, in particular, to this passage:

> *Our success in this war is often measured by the things that did not happen. We cannot know the full extent of the attacks that we and our allies have prevented, but here is some of what we do know: We stopped an al-Qaeda plot to fly a hijacked airplane into the tallest building on the West Coast. We broke up a Southeast Asian terror cell grooming operatives for attacks inside the United States. We uncovered an al-Qaeda cell developing anthrax to be used in attacks against America. And just last August, British authorities uncovered a plot to blow up passenger planes bound for America over the Atlantic Ocean.*

Each of these instances surely vindicated the president's strategy of "taking the fight to the enemy." Alas, not one of them held up to close scrutiny.

———

WEST YORKSHIRE in England has a new chief police constable.

Upon his appointment, Sir Norman Bettison made one of the strangest comments of the year:

"The threat of terrorism," he says, "is lurking out there like *Jaws 2*."

Sir Norman did not exactly mine the richest ore for his analogy of warning. A critic once said of the flopping sequel to the classic film, "You're gonna need a better screenplay."

But this obscure British police official has reminded us that terrorism is still being sold to the public in that country—and in this—as if it were a thrilling horror movie and we were the naughty teenagers about to be its victims.

And it underscores the fact that President Bush took this tack, exactly a week ago tonight, in his terror-related passage in the State of the Union.

A passage that was almost lost amid all the talk about Iraq and health care and bipartisanship and the fellow who saved the stranger from an oncoming subway train in New York City.

But a passage ludicrous and deceitful. Frightening in its hollow conviction. Frightening, in that the president who spoke it tried for *Jaws* but got *Jaws 2*.

I am indebted to David Swanson, press secretary for Dennis Kucinich's 2004 presidential campaign, who has blogged about the dubious ninety-six words in Mr. Bush's address this year and who has concluded that of the four counterterror claims the president made, he went 0-for-4.

"We cannot know the full extent of the attacks that we and our allies have prevented," Mr. Bush noted, "but here is some of what we do know: We stopped an al-Qaeda plot to fly a hijacked airplane into the tallest building on the West Coast."

This would, of course, sir, be the purported plot to knock down the seventy-three-story building in Los Angeles, the one once known as the

Library Tower—the one you personally revealed so breathlessly a year ago next month.

It was embarrassing enough that you mistakenly referred to the structure as the "Liberty Tower."

But within hours it was also revealed that authorities in Los Angeles had had no idea you were going to make any of the details—whether serious or fanciful—public.

Who terrorized Southern California that day, Mr. Bush?

A year ago next month, the *Los Angeles Times* quoted a source—identified only by the labyrinthine description "a U.S. official familiar with the operational aspects of the war on terrorism"—who insisted that the purported "Library Tower plot" was one of many al-Qaeda operations that had not gotten very far past the conceptual stage.

The former staff director of counterterrorism for the National Security Council—now a news analyst for NBC News and MSNBC—Roger Cressey, puts it a little more bluntly.

In our conversation, he put the "Library Tower story" into a category he called the "What-Ifs"—as in the old *Saturday Night Live* sketches that tested the range of comic absurdity:

What if Superman had worked for the Nazis?

What if Spartacus had had a Piper Cub during the battle against the Romans in 70 B.C.?

More ominously, the *L.A. Times* source who debunked the Library Tower story said that those who could correctly measure the flimsiness of the scheme "feared political retaliation for providing a different characterization of the plan than that of the president."

But, Mr. Bush, you're The Decider. And you decided that the Library Tower story should be scored as one for you.

And you continued with a second dubious claim of counterterror success. "We broke up a Southeast Asian terror cell grooming operatives for attacks inside the United States," you said.

Well, sir, you've apparently stumped the intelligence community completely with this one. In his article, Mr. Swanson suggests that in the last week there has been no reporting even hinting at what exactly you were talking about. He hypothesizes that either you were claiming credit for a ring broken up in 1995, or that this was just the Library Tower story "by another name."

Another CIA source suggests to NBC News that since the Southeast Asian cell dreamed of a series of attacks on the same day, you declared the Library Tower one threat thwarted, and all their other ideas a second threat thwarted.

Our colleague Mr. Cressey sums it up: This "Southeast Asian cell" was indeed the tale of the Library Tower, simply repeated. Repeated, Mr. Bush, in consecutive sentences in the State of the Union—in your constitutionally mandated status report on the condition and safety of the nation.

You showed us the same baby twice and claimed it was twins. And then you said that was two for you.

Your third claim, sir, read thusly: "We uncovered an al-Qaeda cell developing anthrax to be used in attacks against America."

Again, the professionals in counterintelligence were startled to hear about this.

Last fall, two *Washington Post* articles cited sources in the FBI and other governmental agencies who said that hopes by foreign terrorists to use anthrax in this country were fanciful at best, farcical at worst. And every effort to link the 2001 anthrax mailings in this country to foreign sources has also struck out. The entire investigation is barely still active.

Mr. Cressey goes a little further. Anything that might even resemble an al-Qaeda cell "developing anthrax," he says, was in the "dreaming" stages. He used as a parallel those pathetic arrests outside Miami last year in which a few men wound up getting charged as terrorists because they couldn't tell the difference between an al-Qaeda operative and an FBI informant. Their "ringleader" seemed to be much more interested in getting his "terrorist masters" to buy him a new car than in actually terrorizing anybody.

That's three for you, Mr. Bush.

"And just last August," you concluded, "British authorities uncovered a plot to blow up passenger planes bound for America over the Atlantic Ocean." In a series of dramatic raids, twenty-four men were arrested.

Turned out, sir, a few of them actually had gone on the Internets* to check out some flight schedules.

Turned out, sir, only a few of them actually had the passports needed to even get on the planes.

The plot to which President Bush referred was a plot without bombs. It was a plot without any indication that the essence of the operation—the in-flight mixing of volatile chemicals carried on board in sports drink bottles—was even doable by amateurs or professional chemists. It was a plot even without sufficient probable cause. One-third of the twenty-four arrested that day—exactly ninety days before the American midterm elections—have since been released.

The British had been watching those men for a year.

Before the week was out, their first statement, that the plot was "ready to go, in days," had been rendered inoperative. British officials told NBC News of the lack of passports and plans; told us that they had wanted to keep the suspects under surveillance for at least another week. Even an American official confirmed to NBC's investigative unit that there was "disagreement over the timing."

The British then went further. Sources inside their government told the English newspaper *The Guardian* that the raids had occurred only because the Pakistanis had arrested a man named Rasheed Raouf. That Raouf had been arrested by Pakistan only because we had threatened to do it for them. That the British had acted only because our government

---

*In keeping with the president's pluralizing of the Web during the 2004 debate, I often refer, on air, to "the Internets."

was willing—to quote that newspaper, *The Guardian*—to "ride rough-shod" over the plans of British intelligence.

Oh, by the way, Mr. Bush, an antiterrorism court in Pakistan reduced the charges against Mr. Raouf to possession of bomb-making materials and being there without proper documents.

Still, sir—evidently, that's close enough.

Score four for you!

Your totally black-and-white conclusions in the State of the Union were based on one gray area, and on three palettes on which the experts can't even see smudge, let alone gray.

It would all be laughable, Mr. Bush, were you not the president of the United States.

It would all be political hyperbole, Mr. Bush, if you had not, on this kind of "intelligence," taken us to war, now sought to escalate that war, and are threatening new war in Iran and maybe even elsewhere.

What you gave us a week ago tonight, sir, was not intelligence, but rather a walk-through of how speculation and innuendo, guesswork and paranoia, daydreaming and fearmongering, combine in your mind and the minds of your government into proof of your derring-do and your success against the terrorists.

The ones who didn't have anthrax.

The ones who didn't have plane tickets or passports.

The ones who didn't have any clue, let alone any plots.

But they go now into our history books as the four terror schemes you've interrupted since 9/11. They go into the collective consciousness as firm evidence of your diligence, of the necessity of your ham-handed treatment of our liberties, of the unavoidability of the 3,075 Americans dead in Iraq.

Congratulations, sir. You are the hero of *Jaws 2*.

You have kept the Piper Cub out of the hands of Spartacus.

17

Condi Goes Too Far

February 26, 2007

On *Fox News Sunday* on February 25, 2007, Secretary of State Condoleezza Rice, whom one might expect to know better, one-upped her colleagues in the competition to make the most outrageous historical claim. Advocates, historians, Jews and gentiles, indeed all other people above the age of six, know that you handle comparisons to Nazis, or their defeat, as you would plutonium. It may be of great use and entirely necessary, but you simply don't throw it against the wall just to see if it sticks.

WE ALREADY KNOW about her suggestion that the president could just ignore whatever congressional Democrats do about Iraq.

Just ignore Congress.

We know how that game always turns out. Ask President Nixon. Ask President Andrew Johnson.

Or ask Vice President Dick Cheney, who utterly contradicted Secretary Rice on Monday when he warned President Pervez Musharraf of Pakistan about what those mean congressional Democrats could do to his foreign aid.

All of this, par for the course.

But about what the secretary said regarding the prospect of Congress's revising or repealing the 2002 authorization of the war in Iraq:

Here we go again! From springs spent trying to link Saddam Hussein to 9/11, to summers of cynically manipulated intelligence, through autumns of false patriotism, to winters of war, we have had more than four years of every cheap trick and every degree of calculated cynicism from this administration filled with three-card monte players.

But the longer Dr. Rice and these other pickpockets of a nation's goodness have walked among us, waving flags and slandering opponents and making true enemies—foreign and domestic—all hat and no cattle all the while, the overriding truth of their occupancy of our highest offices of state has only gradually become clear.

As they asked in that Avis commercial: "Ever get the feeling some people just stopped trying?"

Then defense secretary Donald Rumsfeld thought he could equate those who doubted him with Nazi appeasers, without reminding anybody that the actual, historical Nazi appeasers in this country in the 1930s were the Republicans.

Vice President Cheney thought he could talk as if he and he alone knew the "truth" about Iraq and 9/11, without anyone ever noticing that even the rest of the administration officially disagreed with him.

The president really acted as if you could scare all of the people all of the time and not lose your soul—and your majority—as a result.

But Secretary of State Rice may have now taken the cake. On the Sunday morning interview show of (broken) record on Fox, Dr. Rice spoke a paragraph which, if it had been included in a remedial history paper at the weakest high school in the nation, would've gotten the writer an F—maybe an expulsion.

If Congress were now to revise the Iraq authorization, she said, out loud, with an adult present, "it would be like saying that after Adolf Hitler was overthrown, we needed to change, then, the resolution that allowed the United States to do that, so that we could deal with creating a stable environment in Europe after he was overthrown."

The secretary's résumé reads that she has a master's degree and a Ph.D. in political science. The interviewer should have demanded to see them on the spot. Dr. Rice spoke forty-two words. She may have made more mistakes in them than did the president in his State of the Union address in 2003.

There is, obviously, no mistaking Saddam Hussein for a human being. But nor is there any mistaking him for Adolf Hitler.

Invoking the German dictator who subjugated Europe, who tried to exterminate the Jews, who sought to overtake the world, is not just in the poorest of taste, but in its hyperbole, it insults not merely the victims of the Third Reich, but those in this country who fought it and defeated it.

Saddam Hussein was not Adolf Hitler. And George W. Bush is not Franklin D. Roosevelt—nor Dwight D. Eisenhower. He isn't even George H. W. Bush, who fought in that war.

However, even through the clouds of deliberately spread fear, and even under the weight of a thousand exaggerations of the five years past, one can just barely make out how a battle against international terrorism in 2007 could be compared—by some—to the Second World War.

The analogy is weak, and it instantly begs the question of why those of "The Greatest Generation" focused on Hitler and Hirohito, but our leaders seem to have ignored their vague parallels of today to instead concentrate on the Mussolinis of modern terrorism.

But in some small "You didn't fail, Junior, but you may need to go to summer school" kind of way, you can just make out that comparison.

But, Secretary Rice, overthrowing Saddam Hussein was akin to overthrowing Adolf Hitler? Are you kidding? Did you want to provoke the world's laughter?

And, please, Madam Secretary, if you are going to make that most im-plausible, subjective, dubious, ridiculous comparison—if you want to be as far off the mark about the Second World War as, say, the pathetic Holocaust-denier from Iran, Ahmadinejad—at least get the easily verifi-able facts right: the facts whose home through history lies in your own department.

"The resolution that allowed the United States to" overthrow Hitler?

On the eleventh of December, 1941, at eight o'clock in the morning, two of Hitler's diplomats walked up to the State Department—your of-fice, Secretary Rice—and ninety minutes later they were handing a dec-laration of war to the chief of the department's European Division. The Japanese had bombed Pearl Harbor four days earlier, and the Germans simply piled on.

Your predecessors, Dr. Rice, didn't spend a year making up phony ev-idence and mistaking German balloon-inflating trucks for mobile germ warfare labs. They didn't pretend the world was ending because a tin-pot tyrant couldn't hand over the chemical weapons it turned out he'd de-stroyed a decade earlier. The Germans walked up to the front door of our State Department and said, "We're at war." It was in all the papers. And when that war ended, more than three horrible years later, our troops and the Russians were in Berlin. And we stayed, as an occupying force, well into the 1950s. As an occupying force, Madam Secretary!

If you want to compare what we did to Hitler and in Germany to what we did to Saddam and in Iraq, I'm afraid you're going to have to buy the whole analogy. We were an occupying force in Germany, Dr. Rice, and by your logic, we're now an occupying force in Iraq. And if that's the way you see it, you damn well better come out and tell the American people so. Save your breath telling it to the Iraqis—most of them already buy that part of the comparison.

"It would be like saying that after Adolf Hitler was overthrown, we needed to change, then, the resolution that allowed the United States to do that, so that we could deal with creating a stable environment in Europe after he was overthrown."

We already have a subjectively false comparison between Hitler and Saddam. We already have a historically false comparison between Germany and Iraq. We already have blissful ignorance by our secretary of state about how this country got into the war against Hitler. But then there's this part about changing "the resolution" about Iraq; that it would be as ridiculous in the secretary's eyes as saying that after Hitler was defeated, we needed to go back to Congress to "deal with creating a stable environment in Europe after he was overthrown."

Oh, good grief, Secretary Rice, that's exactly what we did do! We went back to Congress to deal with creating a stable environment in Europe after Hitler was overthrown! It was called the Marshall Plan.

Marshall! General George Catlett Marshall! Secretary of state! The job you have now! C'mon!

Twelve billion four hundred thousand dollars to stabilize all of Europe economically—to keep the next enemies of freedom, the Russians, out, and democracy in! And how do you suppose that happened? The president of the United States went back to Congress and asked it for a new authorization and for the money. And do you have any idea, Madam Secretary, who opposed him when he did that? The Republicans!

"We've spent enough money in Europe," said Senator Robert Taft of Ohio.

"We've spent enough of our resources," said former president Hoover.

It's time to pull out of there! As they stand up, we'll stand down!

This administration has long thought otherwise, but you can't cherry-pick life—whether life in 2007, or life in the history page marked 1945. You can't keep the facts that fit your prejudices and throw out the ones that destroy your theories. And if you're going to try to do that—if you still want to fool some people into thinking that Saddam was Hitler, and once we gave FDR that blank check in Germany he was no longer subject to the laws of Congress or gravity or physics—at least stop humiliating us.

Get your facts straight. Use the Google!*

You've been on *Fox News Sunday,* Secretary Rice. The Fox network has got another show premiering Tuesday night. You could go on that one, too. It might be a better fit. It's called *Are You Smarter Than a Fifth Grader?*

---

*As we honor his use of "the Internets," so too do we cherish President Bush's respect for what he has called "the Google."

18

DeLay's DeLusions

March 26, 2007

Once again, the equation is simple: You might very well need to use plutonium—or a comparison to Hitler or the Nazis—but you had better be confident of your ability to handle either, or you will wind up watching it burn a hole through your chest. A month after Secretary Rice forgot this golden rule, she was followed into the abyss by another washed-up politician with a grandeur complex: former House majority leader Tom DeLay. The indicted ex–bug killer's comparison was between those who pursued his indictment on criminal conspiracy charges and Hitler. Mr. DeLay later expanded on these remarks in an interview on Boston's WERS, at which time he seemed to be comparing his own fate to that of Jewish victims of the Holocaust:

> *I am so outraged by this whole criminalization of politics. It's not good enough to defeat somebody politically. It's not even good enough to vilify somebody publicly. They have to carpet-bomb you with lies and made-up scandals and false charges and indicting you on laws that don't exist. . . . It's the same thing as I say in my book,*

that the Nazis used. . . . It's the same process. It's the same crimi-nalization of politics. It's the same oppression of people. It's the same destroy people in order to gain power. It may be six million Jews, it may be indicting somebody on laws that don't exist. But it's the same philosophy and it's the same worldview.

No, it isn't, and you're a damn fool, and you remind us once again that your erstwhile nickname "The Hammer" may have been less compli-mentary than you surmised. Remember, Mr. DeLay, that a hammer has a head made of solid metal.

THE QUOTE, with the context sucked out from around it, is astonishing.

In a new book, former Republican leader of the House Tom DeLay writes, "Liberals have finally joined the ranks of scoundrels like Hitler."

But restore the context, as with anything else, and you change the meaning of any quote.

In this case, you make it worse.

Mr. DeLay is comparing how he's been treated to how the world was treated by Hitler and the Nazis.

The book is called *No Retreat, No Surrender: One American's Fight.* It has been officially out for nearly two weeks, and it has not cracked the *New York Times* top thirty.

So the fact of this one quotation, first noted only last week by *The Jewish Daily Forward,* could have easily slipped through the cracks.

But even though nobody seems to be reading his book, Mr. DeLay is nonetheless referring to what he calls a lie—the accusation that he vio-lated campaign finance laws in Texas, for which he was indicted.

And on page 156 he writes, "I believe it was Adolf Hitler who first ac-knowledged that the big lie . . ."

Look, stop right there, Mr. DeLay. If you're going to throw around Hitler's name, research the reference, huh? As suggested on The Huffington Post, we have many useful Internet search engines now. If you type "big lie, Hitler" into the one called Google, you get 1,320,000 results.

> I believe it was Adolf Hitler who first acknowledged that the big lie is more effective than the little lie, because the big lie is so audacious, such an astonishing immorality, that people have a hard time believing anyone would say it if it wasn't true.
>
> You know, the big lie—like the Holocaust never happened or dark-skinned people are less intelligent than light-skinned people. Well, by charging this big lie about money laundering, liberals have finally joined the ranks of scoundrels like Hitler.

Okay, where do we start here?

Let's try the gentlest interpretation: Mr. DeLay believes that the accusation that he violated Texas campaign finance laws is on some kind of par with claims that light-skinned people are more intelligent than dark-skinned people.

Now that's the gentlest one.

The somewhat less kind interpretation? He's equating anybody charging him—just him—with anything, even if it were a lie, with the Nazis.

Just by going after Tom DeLay, you are like that old "scoundrel" Hitler.

So Tom DeLay is as important as—what?—democracy in 1930s Germany?

Poland in 1939?

The Jewish people?

So, Mr. DeLay, go back to your Google and type in the name "Tom DeLay" and the phrase "delusions of grandeur."

And you get 11,500 results.

19

Republicans Equal Life,
Democrats Equal Death?

April 25, 2007

Rudy Giuliani had about six good weeks.

He took off his politician mask, and the one beneath it of fearless prosecutor, and he acted like the rest of us did in the New York of September and October 2001. His friends were dead and his heart was broken, and he didn't pretend otherwise. And we thanked him for it. And then he snapped back into political mode and surveyed the ocean of post-traumatic stress disorder around him and "volunteered" to stay on as mayor for a few months after his term was mandated by law to expire. And a lot of us—good grief, I even felt that way for a while— were willing to go along with the most naked attempt to change the inviolability of the election laws in the history of this country, until we were reminded that, hell, in the middle of the Civil War, even Abraham Lincoln stood for reelection, and came damn close to not getting it.

A lot of us—to use Mr. Lincoln's words—disenthralled ourselves about Mr. Giuliani in the weeks, months, and years to come. The sleazy end of Bernard Kerik certainly awakened many of the sleepwalkers.

I myself had been reminded of my first meeting with the mayor of New York, in the mid-nineties. I had been invited by his deputy mayor, Fran Reiter, to be the master of ceremonies for a brief welcoming event on the steps of City Hall for three dozen or so members of baseball's Hall of Fame, who were to be honored again at a dinner that night. I and a few colleagues left ESPN at the crack of dawn to get to the ceremony, and the larger-than-life Ms. Reiter introduced me to Mr. Giuliani. "Mr. Mayor," she bellowed, "this is Keith Olbermann. He's the emcee. He's from ESPN."

What could very well have been a robot in the form of Rudy Giuliani stared back at me through cloudy eyes. "You're Keith Olbermann, you're the emcee, you're from ESPN." I agreed with him that I was. He looked very pleased. Deputy Mayor Reiter led him away.

As the head of the Hall of Fame prepared to introduce Giuliani, he and I were sitting side by side in the front row, looking out at several hundred passersby. I'd already noticed that the microphone at the podium was, atypically, omnidirectional. The mayor, now sitting a few feet from it, coughed—and the cough echoed softly out of the public address system speakers. Giuliani leaned over to me and whispered: "You're Keith Olbermann, you're the emcee, you're from ESPN." I agreed with him again, and he beamed.

The Hall of Fame executive introduced him and the mayor was off and running. He took credit for the beautiful day. He took credit for the strong early-season starts by the Yankees and Mets. He remembered that when he was a kid New York had three teams, the Yankees and Dodgers and Giants, and if he'd been mayor then, they'd all still be here, and then we'd have *four* teams and they'd all be doing well and that would be his doing too and now he'd like to turn it over to . . .

And here the mayor blanked.

He turned helplessly to Deputy Mayor Reiter and mumbled something like "I forgot his name."

My ESPN friends, and others in the audience, laughed.

Fran Reiter detonated. She needed no super-efficient microphone. "You *said* you'd *remember*! You *repeated it for me*! Olbermann! Keith Olbermann! He's the emcee, from ESPN!"

Behind me, Hall of Famer Al Kaline laughed (I think sympathetically).

Giuliani turned back to the crowd. "Right. Let me introduce our encee from ESPM, Keith Obleman . . ."

Kaline's laugh was not sympathetic. Nor were those of my friends in the crowd.

For me, time slowed. I thought only of revenge. Get to my feet and say "Thank you, Mayor Dinkins? Mayor Koch? Mayor La Guardia?" Able ripostes, no doubt. But I was here representing ESPN and under the auspices of the Hall of Fame, and my disrespect would become their disrespect. So I just sat there and made Mayor Zombie reintroduce me. As Reiter stage-whispered my name correctly, Rudy came slightly closer to it.

There is some belief that this anecdote captures the essence of Giuliani: a kind of mechanical man who comes to attention only in the presence of a large crowd of followers and who may or may not be aware of what he is saying. In April 2007 I began to suspect this was the kindest interpretation. Mr. Giuliani took a page from George Bush's playbook of the previous fall, and decided that not only were the Democrats soft on "terror," but all other Republicans were, too.

I guess the real test of Mr. Giuliani's hopes for the White House is to ask him if he can remember the *names* of those other Republicans and Democrats.

SINCE SOME indeterminable hour between the final dousing of the pyre at the World Trade Center and the breaking of what Senator Barack Obama has aptly termed "9/11 fever," it has been profoundly and disturbingly evident that we are at the center of one of history's great ironies.

Only in this America of the early twenty-first century could it be true that the man who was president during the worst attack on our nation and the man who was the mayor of the city in which that attack principally unfolded would not only be absolved of any and all blame for the unreadiness of their own governments, but, moreover, would thereafter be branded heroes of those attacks.

And now, that mayor—whose most profound municipal act in the wake of that nightmare was to suggest the postponement of the election to select his own successor—has gone even a step beyond these M. C. Escher constructions of history.

"If any Republican is elected president—and I think obviously I would be best at this—we will remain on offense and will anticipate what [the terrorists] will do and try to stop them before they do it."

Insisting that the election of any Democrat would mean the country was "back . . . on defense," Mr. Giuliani continued: "But the question is how long will it take and how many casualties will we have. If we are on defense, we will have more losses and it will go on longer."

He said this with no sense of irony, no sense of any personal shortcomings, no sense whatsoever.

And if you somehow missed what he was really saying, somehow didn't hear the none-too-subtle subtext of "Vote Democratic and die," Mr. Giuliani then stripped away any barrier of courtesy, telling Roger Simon of politico.com:

"America will be safer with a Republican president."

At least that Republican president under which we have not been safer has, even at his worst, maintained some microscopic distance between himself and a campaign platform that blithely threatened the American people with "casualties" if they, next year, elect a Democratic president—or, inferring from Mr. Giuliani's flights of grandeur in New Hampshire, even if they elect a different Republican.

How—dare—you, sir?

"How many casualties will we have?" This is the language of Osama bin Laden.

Yours, Mr. Giuliani, is the same chilling nonchalance of the madman, of the proselytizer who has moved even from some crude framework of politics and society into a virtual Roman Colosseum of carnage, and a conceit over your own ability—and worthiness—to decide who lives and who dies.

Rather than a reasoned discussion—rather than a political campaign advocating your own causes and extolling your own qualifications—you have bypassed all the intermediate steps and moved directly to trying to terrorize the electorate into viewing a vote for a Democrat not as a reasonable alternative and an inalienable right—but as an act of suicide.

This is not the mere politicizing of Iraq, nor the vague mumbled epithets about Democratic "softness" from a delusional vice president.

This is casualties on a partisan basis—of the naked assertion that Mr. Giuliani's party knows all and will save those who have voted for it, and to hell with everybody else. And that he, with no foreign policy experience whatsoever, is somehow the messiah of the moment.

Even to grant that that formula—whether posed by Republican or Democrat—is somehow not the most base, the most indefensible, the most un-American electioneering in our history—even if it is somehow acceptable to assign "casualties" to one party and "safety" to the other—even if we have become so profane in our thinking that it is part of our political vocabulary to view counterterror as one party's property and the other's liability—on what imaginary track record does Mr. Giuliani base his boast?

Which party held the presidency on September 11, 2001, Mr. Giuliani?

Which party held the mayoralty of New York on that date, Mr. Giuliani?

Which party assured New Yorkers that the air was safe and the remains of the dead recovered and not being used to fill potholes, Mr. Giuliani?

Which party wanted what the terrorists wanted—the postponement of elections—and to whose personal advantage would that have redounded, Mr. Giuliani?

Which mayor of New York was elected eight months after the first attack on the World Trade Center, yet did not emphasize counterterror in the same city for the next eight years, Mr. Giuliani?

Which party had proposed to turn over the Department of Homeland Security to Bernard Kerik, Mr. Giuliani? Who wanted to ignore and hide Kerik's organized crime allegations, Mr. Giuliani? Who personally argued to the White House that Kerik need not be vetted, Mr. Giuliani?

Which party rode roughshod over Americans' rights while braying that it was actually protecting them, Mr. Giuliani?

Which party took this country into the most utterly backwards, utterly counterproductive, utterly ruinous war in our history, Mr. Giuliani?

Which party has been in office as more Americans were killed in the pointless fields of Iraq than were killed in the consuming nightmare of 9/11, Mr. Giuliani?

Drop this argument, sir. You will lose it.

"The Democrats do not understand the full nature and scope of the terrorist war against us," Mr. Giuliani continued to the Rockingham County Lincoln Day Dinner last night. "Never, ever again will this country be on defense waiting for [terrorists] to attack us, if I have anything to say about it. And make no mistake, the Democrats want to put us back on defense."

There is no room for this. This is terrorism itself, dressed up as counterterrorism.

It is not warning, but bullying—substituted for the political discourse now absolutely essential to this country's survival and the freedom of its people.

No Democrat has said words like these. None has ever campaigned on the Republicans' flat-footedness of September 11, 2001. None has the requisite irresponsible, all-consuming ambition. None is willing to say "I accuse" rather than recognize that, to some degree, all of us share responsibility for our collective stupor.

And if it is somehow insufficient that this is morally, spiritually, and politically wrong, to screech as Mr. Giuliani has screeched, there is also this: that gaping hole in Mr. Giuliani's argument of "Republicans equal life, Democrats equal death."

Not only have the Republicans not lived up to their babbling on this subject, but last fall the electorate called them on it. As doubtless they would call you on it, Mr. Giuliani.

Repeat—go beyond—Mr. Bush's rhetorical calamities of 2006.

Call attention to the casualties on your watch, and your long waking slumber in the years between the two attacks on the World Trade Center.

Become the candidate who runs on the Vote-for-Me-or-Die platform.

Do a Joe McCarthy, a Lyndon Johnson, a Robespierre.

Only, if you choose so to do, do not come back surprised nor remorseful if the voters remind you that "terror" is not just a matter of "casualties." It is, just as surely, a matter of the promulgation of fear.

Claim a difference between the parties on the voters' chances of survival—and you do bin Laden's work for him.

And we—Democrats and Republicans alike, and every variation in between—we Americans!—are sick to death of you and the other terror-mongers trying to frighten us into submission, into the surrender of our rights and our reason, into this betrayal of that for which this country has always stood.

Franklin Roosevelt's words ring true again tonight. And, clarified and amplified, they are just as current now as they were when first he spoke them, seventy-four years ago.

"We have nothing to fear but fear itself"—and those who would exploit our fear, for power and for their own personal, selfish, cynical gain.

20

The Entire Government Has Failed Us on Iraq

May 23, 2007

I'm frequently accused of being a liberal, or a flack for the Democratic Party. And it's true that the vast majority of my commentary over these past few years has targeted Republicans. But if the job of journalists in a democracy is to hold the powerful accountable, then it makes sense that one would focus on those who have had the majority of the power in the most recent historical time frame. That, of course, would be a Republican president and a Republican Congress. The midterm elections obviously changed this picture, and this Special Comment marked my first, though I fear not my last, attempt to hold the newly elected Democratic majority accountable when it appears to have conceded on the very issue on which it was elected.

THIS IS, IN FACT, a comment about—betrayal.

Few men or women elected in our history—whether executive or legislative, state or national—have been sent into office with a mandate more obvious, nor instructions more clear: *Get us out of Iraq.*

Yet after six months of preparation and execution—half a year gathering the strands of public support, translating into action the collective will of the nearly 70 percent of Americans who reject this War of Lies—the Democrats have managed only this:

- The Democratic leadership has surrendered to a president—if not the worst president, then easily the most selfish, in our history—who happily blackmails his own people, and uses his own military personnel as hostages to his asinine demand that the Democrats "give the troops their money";
- The Democratic leadership has agreed to finance the deaths of Americans in a war that has only reduced the security of Americans;
- The Democratic leadership has given Mr. Bush all that he wanted, with the only caveat being not merely meaningless symbolism about benchmarks for the Iraqi government, but *optional* meaningless symbolism about benchmarks for the Iraqi government.
- The Democratic leadership has, in sum, claimed a compromise with the administration in which the only things truly compromised are the trust of the voters, the ethics of the Democrats, and the lives of our brave, and doomed, friends and family in Iraq.

You, the men and women elected with the simplest of directions—*Stop the war*—have traded your strength, your bargaining position, and the uniform support of those who elected you—for a handful of magic beans.

You may trot out every political cliché from the soft-soap, inside-the-beltway dictionary of boilerplate sound bites about how this is the "beginning of the end" of Mr. Bush's "carte blanche" in Iraq, about how this is a "first step."

Well, Senator Reid, the only end at its beginning is our collective hope that you and your colleagues would do what is right, what is essential, what you were each elected and reelected to do.

Because this "first step" . . . is a step right off a cliff.

And this president!

How shameful it would be to watch an adult hold his breath and threaten to continue to do so until he turned blue.

But how horrifying it is to watch a president hold his breath and threaten to continue to do so until innocent and patriotic Americans in harm's way are bled white.

You lead this country, sir? You claim to defend it?

And yet when faced with the prospect of someone calling you on your stubbornness—your stubbornness which has cost 3,431 Americans their lives and thousands more their limbs—you, Mr. Bush, imply that if the Democrats don't give you the money and give it to you entirely on your terms, the troops in Iraq will be stranded, or forced to serve longer, or have to throw bullets at the enemy with their bare hands.

How transcendentally, how historically, pathetic.

Any other president from any other moment in the panorama of our history would have, at the outset of this tawdry game of political chicken, declared that no matter what the other political side did, he would ensure personally—first, last, and always—that the troops would not suffer.

A president, Mr. Bush, uses the carte blanche he has already, not to manipulate an overlap of arriving and departing brigades into a "second surge," but to say in unequivocal terms that if it takes every last dime of the moneys already allocated, if it takes reneging on government contracts with Halliburton, he will make sure the troops are safe—even if the only safety to be found is in getting them the hell out of there.

Well, any true president would have done that, sir.

You, instead, used our troops as political pawns, then blamed the Democrats when you did so.

Not that these Democrats, who had this country's support and sympathy up until forty-eight hours ago, have not since earned all the blame they can carry home.

"We seem to be very near the bleak choice between war and shame," Winston Churchill wrote to Lord Moyne in the days after the British signed the Munich accords with Germany in 1938. "My feeling is that we shall choose shame, and then have war thrown in, a little later."

That's what this is for the Democrats, isn't it? Their "Neville Chamberlain moment" before the Second World War.

All that's missing is the landing at the airport, with the blinkered leader waving a piece of paper which he naïvely thought would guarantee "peace in our time," but which his opponent would ignore with deceit.

The Democrats have merely streamlined the process.

Their piece of paper already says Mr. Bush can ignore it, with impunity.

And where are the Democratic presidential hopefuls this evening?

See they not that to which the Senate and House leadership has blinded itself?

Judging these candidates based on how they voted on the original Iraq authorization, or waiting for apologies for those votes, is ancient history now.

The Democratic nomination is likely to be decided tomorrow.

The talk of practical politics, the buying-into of the president's dishonest construction "Fund the troops or they will be in jeopardy," the promise of tougher action in September, is falling not on deaf ears, but rather falling on Americans who already told you what to do and now perceive your ears as closed to practical politics.

Those who seek the Democratic nomination need to—for their own political futures and, with a thousand times more solemnity and importance, for the individual futures of our troops—denounce this betrayal, vote against it, and, if need be, unseat Majority Leader Reid and Speaker

Pelosi if they continue down this path of guilty, fatal acquiescence to the tragically misguided will of a monomaniacal president.

For, ultimately, at this hour, the entire government has failed us.

- Mr. Reid, Mr. Hoyer, and the other Democrats have failed us. They negotiated away that which they did not own, but had only been entrusted by us to protect: our collective will as the citizens of this country, that this brazen War of Lies be ended as rapidly and safely as possible.
- Mr. Bush and his government have failed us. They have behaved venomously and without dignity—of course. That is all at which Mr. Bush is gifted. We are the ones providing any element of surprise or shock here.
- With the exception of Senator Dodd and Senator Edwards, the Democratic presidential candidates have (so far at least) failed us. They must now speak, and make plain how they view what has been given away to Mr. Bush, and what is yet to be given away tomorrow, and in the thousand tomorrows to come.

Because for the next fourteen months, the Democratic nominating process—indeed, the whole of our political discourse until further notice—has, with the stroke of a cursed pen, become about one thing, and one thing alone.

The electorate figured this out six months ago. The president and the Republicans have not—doubtless will not. The Democrats will figure it out during the Memorial Day recess, when they go home and many of those who elected them will politely suggest they stay there—and permanently.

Because, on the subject of Iraq, the people have been ahead of the media—

Ahead of the government—

Ahead of the politicians—

For the last year, or two years, or maybe three.

Our politics is now about the answer to one briefly worded question.

Mr. Bush has failed.

Mr. Warner has failed.

Mr. Reid has failed.

So.

Who among us will stop this war—this War of Lies?

To him or her fall the figurative keys to the nation.

To all the others—presidents and majority leaders and candidates and rank-and-file congressmen and senators of either party—there is only blame, for this shameful, and bipartisan, betrayal.

21

Bush and Cheney Should Resign

July 3, 2007

I gave this Special Comment the night after President Bush commuted the prison sentence of Lewis "Scooter" Libby, former chief of
staff to Vice President Cheney. As were many Americans, I was outraged by the president's clear statement that our nation's laws don't
apply to rich, powerful, white Republicans. How can a president free
one of his own former employees? How can a president ignore the
courts? How can a president ignore public opinion, even among only
those in his own party? And how can he be so gutless as to not even
make his announcement on camera? A president who lied us into a
war and in so doing needlessly killed more than three thousand of our
family and friends and neighbors, a president whose administration
initially tried to destroy the first man to nail that lie, a president whose
henchmen then ruined the career of the intelligence asset that was his
wife when intelligence assets were never more essential to the viabil-
ity of the republic—a president like that freed from the prospect of
prison the only man ever to come to trial for one of the component

felonies in what may be the greatest crime of this young century, and found a new way to undermine our faith in the institution he had solemnly sworn to faithfully defend.

"I DIDN'T VOTE FOR HIM," an American once said, "but he's my president, and I hope he does a good job."

That—on this eve of the Fourth of July—is the essence of this democracy, in seventeen words. And that is what President Bush threw away yesterday in commuting the sentence of Lewis "Scooter" Libby.

The man who said those seventeen words—improbably enough—was the actor John Wayne. And Wayne, an ultraconservative, said them when he learned of the hair's-breadth election of John F. Kennedy instead of his personal favorite, Richard Nixon, in 1960.

"I didn't vote for him, but he's my president, and I hope he does a good job."

The sentiment was doubtlessly expressed earlier, but there is something especially appropriate about hearing it, now, in Wayne's voice: the crisp, matter-of-fact acknowledgment that we have survived, even though for nearly two centuries now our commander in chief has also served simultaneously as the head of one political party and often the scourge of all others.

We as citizens must, at some point, ignore a president's partisanship. Not that we may prosper as a nation, not that we may achieve, not that we may lead the world—but merely that we may function.

But just as essential to the seventeen words of John Wayne is an implicit trust—a sacred trust: that the president for whom so many did not vote can in turn suspend his political self long enough, and for matters imperative enough, to conduct himself solely for the benefit of the entire republic.

Our generation's willingness to state, "We didn't vote for him, but he's our president, and we hope he does a good job" was tested in the crucible of history, and earlier than most. And in circumstances more tragic and threatening. And we did that with which history tasked us.

We enveloped our president in 2001. And those who did not believe he should have been elected—indeed, those who did not believe he *had* been elected—willingly lowered their voices and assented to the sacred oath of nonpartisanship.

And George W. Bush took our assent, and reconfigured it, and honed it, and shaped it to a razor-sharp point and stabbed this nation in the back with it.

Were there any remaining lingering doubt otherwise, or any remaining lingering hope, it ended yesterday when Mr. Bush commuted the prison sentence of one of his own staffers. Did so even before the appeals process was complete; did so without as much as a courtesy consultation with the Department of Justice; did so despite what James Madison—at the Constitutional Convention—said about impeaching any president who pardoned or sheltered those who had committed crimes "advised by" that president; did so without the slightest concern that even the most detached of citizens must look at the chain of events and wonder, to what degree was Mr. Libby told: Break the law however you wish—the president will keep you out of prison?

In that moment, Mr. Bush, you broke that fundamental compact between yourself and the majority of this nation's citizens—the ones who did not cast votes for you. In that moment, Mr. Bush, you ceased to be the president of the United States. In that moment, Mr. Bush, you became merely the president of a rabid and irresponsible corner of the Republican Party. And this is too important a time, sir, to have a commander in chief who puts party over nation.

This has been, of course, the gathering legacy of this administration. Few of its decisions have escaped the stain of politics. The extraordinary Karl Rove has spoken of "a permanent Republican majority," as if such a thing—or a permanent Democratic majority—is not antithetical to that upon which rest our country, our history, our revolution, our freedoms.

Yet our democracy has survived shrewder men than Karl Rove. And it has survived the frequent stain of politics upon the fabric of government. But this administration, with ever-increasing insistence and almost theocratic zealotry, has turned that stain into a massive oil spill.

The protection of the environment is turned over to those of one political party, who will financially benefit from the rape of the environment. The protections of the Constitution are turned over to those of one political party, who believe those protections unnecessary and extravagant and quaint.

The enforcement of the laws is turned over to those of one political party, who will swear beforehand that they will not enforce those laws. The choice between war and peace is turned over to those of one political party, who stand to gain vast wealth by ensuring that there is never peace, but only war.

And now, when just one cooked book gets corrected by an honest auditor, when just one trampling of the inherent and inviolable fairness of government is rejected by an impartial judge, when just one wild-eyed partisan is stopped by the figure of blind justice, this president decides that he, and not the law, must prevail.

I accuse you, Mr. Bush, of lying this country into war.

I accuse you of fabricating in the minds of your own people a false implied link between Saddam Hussein and 9/11.

I accuse you of firing the generals who told you that the plans for Iraq were disastrously insufficient.

I accuse you of causing in Iraq the needless deaths of 3,586 of our brothers and sons, and sisters and daughters, and friends and neighbors.

I accuse you of subverting the Constitution, not in some misguided but sincerely motivated struggle to combat terrorists, but to stifle dissent.

I accuse you of fomenting fear among your own people, of creating the very terror you claim to have fought.

I accuse you of exploiting that unreasoning fear, the natural fear of your own people who just want to live their lives in peace, as a political tool to slander your critics and libel your opponents.

I accuse you of handing part of this republic over to a vice president who is without conscience and letting him run roughshod over it.

And I accuse you now, Mr. Bush, of giving, through that vice president, carte blanche to Mr. Libby, to help defame Ambassador Joseph Wilson by any means necessary, to lie to grand juries and special counsel and before a court, in order to protect the mechanisms and particulars of that defamation, with your guarantee that Libby would never see prison, and in so doing, as Ambassador Wilson himself phrased it here last night, of becoming an accessory to the obstruction of justice.

When President Nixon ordered the firing of the Watergate special prosecutor Archibald Cox during the infamous "Saturday Night Massacre" on October 20, 1973, Cox initially responded, tersely and ominously, "Whether ours shall be a government of laws and not of men, is now for Congress, and ultimately, the American people."

President Nixon did not understand how he had crystallized the issue of Watergate for the American people. It had been about the obscure meaning behind an attempt to break into a rival party's headquarters, and the labyrinthine effort to cover up that break-in and the related crimes. And in one night, Nixon transformed it. Watergate—instantaneously—became a simpler issue: a president overruling the inexorable march of the law; of insisting—in a way that resonated viscerally with millions who had not previously understood—that he was the law.

Not the Constitution. Not the Congress. Not the courts. Just him.

Just—Mr. Bush—as you did yesterday.

The twists and turns of Plamegate, of your precise and intricate lies that sent us into this bottomless pit of Iraq; your lies upon the lies to discredit Joe Wilson; your lies upon the lies upon the lies to throw the sand at the "referee" of Prosecutor Fitzgerald's analogy—these are complex and often painful to follow, and too much, perhaps, for the average citizen.

But when other citizens render a verdict against your man, Mr. Bush, and then you spit in the faces of those jurors and that judge and the judges who were yet to hear the appeal—the average citizen understands that, sir.

It's the fixed ball game and the rigged casino and the prearranged lottery all rolled into one—and it stinks. And they know it.

Nixon's mistake, the last and most fatal of them—the firing of Archibald Cox—was enough to cost him the presidency. And in the end, even Richard Nixon could say he could not put this nation through an impeachment.

It was far too late for it to matter then, but as the decades unfold, that single final gesture of nonpartisanship, of acknowledged responsibility not to self, not to party, not to "base," but to country, echoes loudly into history. Even Richard Nixon knew it was time to resign.

Would that you could say that, Mr. Bush. And that you could say it for Mr. Cheney. You both crossed the Rubicon yesterday. Which one of you chose the route no longer matters. Which is the ventriloquist and which the dummy is irrelevant.

But that you have twisted the machinery of government into nothing more than a tawdry machine of politics is the only fact that remains relevant.

It is nearly July Fourth, Mr. Bush, the commemoration of the moment we Americans decided that rather than live under a king who made up the laws, or erased them, or ignored them—or commuted the sentences of those rightly convicted under them—we would force our independence and regain our sacred freedoms.

We of this time—and our leaders in Congress, of both parties—must now live up to those standards which echo through our history: Pressure, negotiate, impeach—get you, Mr. Bush, and Mr. Cheney, two men who are now perilous to our democracy, away from its helm.

For you, Mr. Bush, and for Mr. Cheney, there is a lesser task. You need merely achieve a very low threshold indeed. Display just that iota of patriotism which Richard Nixon showed on August 9, 1974.

Resign.

And give us someone—anyone—about whom all of us might yet be able to quote John Wayne and say, "I didn't vote for him, but he's my president, and I hope he does a good job."

22

All Hail the Prophetic Gut!

July 12, 2007

Nothing gets me fired up more quickly than "The Department of Homeland Security."

It carries such an Orwellian connotation: securing our homes, our land, by invading our privacy. Ensuring our safety by scaring the crap out of us. Seeking to lend a tone of sophistication and specialization while being run by an ordinary politician from Pennsylvania, then (abortively) by a corrupt ex–New York City cop, then (most obtusely) by a hack prosecutor from New Jersey. It is the epitome of Orwell's newspeak, with just a dash of that fascist tone provided by the very word "homeland."

It's a word, as I pointed out in this Special Comment from July 2007, that really has no pre-9/11 American roots, and really has no place post-9/11. But we have seen such crap bubble to the surface and be mistaken for cream that perhaps this isn't all that surprising—nor is Michael Chertoff. One of the auteurs of the USA PATRIOT Act, one of the brilliant prosecutors of Zacarias Moussaoui (closer to the Fifth Beatle than the Twentieth Hijacker), Chertoff is the classic apparatchik.

And once again, just after the Fourth of July and just as the Bush administration took another leap backward from credibility, he put his foot in his mouth. But when the supposed head of counterterrorism in this country makes such a gaffe, we can't chortle. Too many of us are too scared, and the rest of us are too angry.

YOU HAVE BY NOW heard the remark—instantly added to our through-the-looking-glass lexicon of the twenty-first century, a time when we suddenly started referring to this country as "the homeland," as if anybody here has used that term since Charles Lindbergh or the German-American Bund in 1940.

Michael Chertoff's "gut feeling."

Which, he took pains to emphasize, was based on no specific nor even vague intelligence that we are entering a period of increased risk of terrorism here.

He got as specific as saying that al-Qaeda seems to like the summer, but as to the rest of it, he is perfectly content to let us sit and wait and worry—and to contemplate his gut.

His gut!

We used to have John Ashcroft's major announcements.

We used to have David Paulison's breathless advisories about how to use duct tape against radiation attacks.

We used to have Tom Ridge's color-coded threat levels.

Now we have Michael Chertoff's gut!

Once, we thought we were tiptoeing along a Grand Canyon of possible and actual freedoms and civil liberties destroyed, as part of some kind of nauseating but ultimately necessary and intricately designed plan to stop future 9/11s or even future Glasgow car bombers who wind up having to get out and push their failed weapons.

Now it turns out we are risking all of our rights and protections—and risking the anger and hatred of the rest of the world—for the sake of Michael Chertoff's gut.

I have pondered this supreme expression of diminished expectations for parts of three days now. I have concluded that there are only five possible explanations for Mr. Chertoff's remarkable revelations about his transcendently important counterterrorism stomach.

Firstly, Mr. Chertoff, you are, as Richard Wolffe said here the other night, actually referencing not your gut but your backside—as in, "covering it." CYA.

Not only has there not been a terrorist attack stopped in this country, but your good old Homeland Security hasn't even unraveled a plausible terrorist plan.

And you and your folks there have a different kind of stomach pain, knowing that with a track record that consists largely of two accomplishments—inconveniencing people at airports and scaring them everywhere else—your department doesn't know what the hell it's doing, and even you, Mr. Chertoff, know it.

Secondly, of course, there is the explanation of choice for those millions of us who have heard the shrill and curiously timed cries of "wolf" over the past six years—what we've called here "the nexus of politics and terror"—that there isn't anything cooking, and your "gut feeling" was actually that you'd better throw up a diversion soon on Mr. Bush's behalf, or something real—like the Republicans' revolt about Iraq, and the nauseating "gut feeling" that we have gotten 3,611 Americans killed there for no reason—was actually going to seep into the American headlines and consciousness.

It's impossible to prove a negative, to guarantee that you and your predecessors deliberately scared the American public just for the political hell of it—even though your predecessor, Mr. Ridge, admitted he had his suspicions about exactly that.

Suffice to say, Mr. Chertoff: If it ever can be proved, there will be a lot of people from Homeland Security and other outposts of this remarkably corrupt administration who will be going to prison.

Thirdly—and most charitably, I guess, Mr. Chertoff—is the possibility that you have made some credible inference that we are really at greater risk right now but that any detail might blow some sort of attempt at interruption. There is some silver lining in this one.

But the silver lining would have been a greater one if this National Counterterrorism Center report hadn't leaked out the day after you introduced us to your gut, a report suggesting al-Qaeda had rebuilt its operational capacity to pre-9/11 levels.

Not only did this latest hair-on-fire missive remind us that al-Qaeda's regrowth has been along the Pakistan-Afghanistan border; not only did it remind us that your boss let this happen by shifting his resources out of Afghanistan to Iraq for his own vain and foolish purposes, to say nothing of ignoring Pakistan; not only did it underscore the ominous truth that if this country is victimized again by al-Qaeda, the personal responsibility for the failure of our misplaced defenses would belong to President Bush and President Bush alone; but on top of all of it, Mr. Chertoff, it revealed you for the phony expert you are—the kid who hears in confidence something smart from somebody smart and then makes his prediction that what the smart kid said confidentially is about to happen. It reads just as you revised the "gut" remark this morning, sir—the "informed opinion." The kid telling stories out of school.

The fourth possibility is a simple reversal of the third, Mr. Chertoff.

You shot off your bazoo, and then this National Counterterrorism Center report was rushed out—even created—to cover you, to give you credibility, to cloud the reality that you actually intoned to the *Chicago Tribune,* the twenty-first-century equivalent of "by the pricking of my thumbs, something wicked this way comes."

But the fifth possible explanation of your gut, Mr. Chertoff, is the real nightmare scenario.

And it is simple.

That you, the man who famously told us "Louisiana is a city that is largely underwater," meant this literally.

That we really have been reduced to listening to see if your gut will growl.

That your intestines are our best defense.

That your bowels are our listening devices, your digestive tract is full of augurs, your colon produces the results that the torture at Gitmo does not.

All hail the prophetic gut!

So there are your choices: bureaucratic self-protection, political manipulation of the worst kind, the dropping of opaque hints, a gaffe backfilled by an "instant report," or the complete disintegration of our counterterror effort.

Even if there really is never another terror attempt in this country, we have already lost too much in these last six years to now have to listen to Michael Chertoff's gut, no matter what its motivation.

We cannot and will not turn this country into a police state. But even those of us who say that most loudly and insistently acknowledge that some stricter measures, under the still stricter supervision of as many watchdogs as we can summon, are appropriate.

But you're not even going to wring any of that from us, Mr. Chertoff, if we're going to hear remarks about your "gut feelings."

You have reduced yourself to the status of a hunch-driven clown, and it's probably time you turned your task over to somebody who represents the brain and not the gut—certainly to somebody who does not, as you do now, represent that other part of the anatomy, the one through which the body disposes of what the stomach doesn't want.

23

Go to Iraq and Fight, Mr. President

July 19, 2007

I've been a fast writer ever since I showed up for something called "Comp Class" at the Hackley School in Tarrytown, New York, in September 1970. It wasn't a theoretical writing course; it was more like learning to swim by being thrown into the surf. True to the brand name, those familiar black-and-white-speckle-covered "composition notebooks" would be handed out, then a topic—or often the dread "free topic"—would be chalked out on a blackboard and an empathetically smirking English teacher would say "Go." We had fifty-five minutes to think up, map out, and write—by hand—three to five pages with the proverbial beginning, middle, and end.

I don't know if I perceived it then, but after five years of that kind of practice, usually at the very start of the school day, the worst of us was fully prepared to skate through almost any writing load that college—or real life—could present us. I can still see a National Merit Scholar from Ohio blanching visibly as she sat opposite me in our first week at Cornell. We'd been assigned three three-page papers as the entire essay total for a semester-long Shakespeare course. I thought, "You want 'em Thursday?" She later admitted to me that at her high school, she'd never written anything longer than three paragraphs.

In my very first job, at UPI Audio, in 1979, I discovered that my "Hackley Comp" training had been surprisingly specific. I had to write and announce a two-minute sportscast once an hour. There were other tasks that ate into the intervals between my minutes in the studio, and the writing was a little less, and (with a typewriter) a little easier. But it still amounted to having fifty-five minutes to write the equivalent of three to five handwritten pages with the proverbial beginning, middle, and end.

This long preamble is offered to explain that I generally *can* write the script of an entire edition of *Countdown*—though I no longer try to, if I can avoid it—and can do so without a second draft. The Special Comments have been different. These are usually composed at home, at night, then read aloud, then slept upon, then rewritten, then read aloud again, then "blocked" (the process by which visual elements and camera changes are selected), and then tinkered with to the point of paranoia. I have revised portions in the commercial breaks that preceded them.

But not this one, which followed the leaking of Under Secretary of Defense Eric Edelman's unconscionable letter to Senator Clinton, after she had asked for details on the Pentagon's plan for evacuating the troops from Iraq. The e-mail traffic suggests I saw it in Los Angeles, on my way back from—of all things—a first reading of a new episode script by the cast of *The Simpsons*—and that this would've been around 2:00 P.M. Eastern time. By 2:45 I was plinking out this Comment in a Beverly Hills hotel room. The initial draft was done by 4:00, and I read it on camera at 8:00 P.M. Eastern. No brooding contemplation here.

I might add that we had unique circumstances that night. Senator John Kerry had already been booked as a guest to discuss a Pentagon briefing of ninety lawmakers that day. When I realized that the Edelman letter smacked of the tactics of the Swift Boat Vets, I knew we had to structure the show to give Kerry a chance to comment. Yet our interview was to be taped at 6:30 Eastern that night. To accomplish all this, and not leave the senator in the dark, we had to send Kerry a copy of my remarks, then record the interview, then open the show with the Comment. He was in fact responding to a commentary I had not yet given, and which he had only seen in print. The senator was gracious and supportive, and I like to think we backstopped each other. He agreed that he'd seen this tactic before, and should've spent more time and money in the 2004 campaign attacking the attacks he then faced. And he echoed what I had written—that it was a wondrous thing that no member of the administration had even hinted at wishing he could fight in Iraq, or send his or her own children there. I was reminded of the old gag by the British radio comedy artists of the 1950s (including Peter Sellers) who called themselves *The Goon Show.* In one scene, two characters were trapped in a prison with a twenty-foot-high window. The first said to the other, "Get up on my shoulders," and sounds of grunting and struggling could be heard. He then said, "Now, I'll get up on *your* shoulders!" More grunting. "Now, you get up on *my* shoulders." So it went in impossible but beautiful fantasy until they escaped. It strikes me that this may be the way we effect political change in this country. You get up on my shoulders, then I'll get up on yours. Just keep believing that it isn't physically impossible, and sooner rather than later, we'll be free.

IT IS ONE of the great, dark, evil lessons of history.

A country—a government—a military machine—can screw up a war seven ways to Sunday. It can get thousands of its people killed. It can risk the safety of its citizens. It can destroy the fabric of its nation.

But as long as it can identify a scapegoat, it can regain or even gain power.

The Bush administration has opened this Pandora's box about Iraq. It has found its scapegoats: Hillary Clinton and us.

The lies and terror tactics with which it deluded this country into war—*they* had nothing to do with the abomination that Iraq has become. It isn't Mr. Bush's fault.

The selection of the wrong war, in the wrong time, in the wrong place—the most disastrous geopolitical tactic since Austria-Hungary attacked Serbia in 1914 and destroyed itself in the process—*that* had nothing to do with the overwhelming crisis Iraq has become. It isn't Mr. Bush's fault.

The criminal lack of planning for the war—the total "jump-off-a-bridge-and-hope-you-can-fly" tone to the failure to anticipate what would follow the deposing of Saddam Hussein—*that* had nothing to do with the chaos in which Iraq has been enveloped. It isn't Mr. Bush's fault.

The utter, blinkered idiocy of "staying the course," of sending Americans to Iraq and sending them a second time, and a third and a fourth, until they get killed or maimed—the utter deprioritization of human life, simply so a politician can avoid having to admit a mistake—*that* had nothing to do with the tens of thousand individual tragedies darkening the lives of American families forever. It isn't Mr. Bush's fault.

The continuing, relentless, remorseless, corrupt, and cynical insistence that this conflict somehow is defeating or containing or just engaging the people who attacked us on 9/11, the total Alice-through-the-looking-glass quality that ignores that in Iraq, we have made the world safer for al-Qaeda—it isn't Mr. Bush's fault!

The fault, brought down as if a sermon from this mount of hypocrisy and slaughter by a nearly anonymous under secretary of defense, has tonight been laid at the doorstep of Senator Hillary Clinton, and, by extension, at the doorstep of every American—the now-vast majority of us—who have dared to criticize this war or protest it or merely ask questions about it or simply, plaintively, innocently, honestly, plead, "Don't take my son, don't take my daughter."

Senator Clinton has been sent—and someone has leaked to the Associated Press—a letter, sent in reply to hers asking if there exists an actual plan for evacuating U.S. troops from Iraq.

This extraordinary document was written by an under secretary of defense named Eric Edelman.

"Premature and public discussion of the withdrawal of U.S. forces from Iraq," Edelman writes, "reinforces enemy propaganda that the United States will abandon its allies in Iraq, much as we are perceived to have done in Vietnam, Lebanon and Somalia." Edelman adds, "Such talk understandably unnerves the very same Iraqi allies we are asking to assume enormous personal risks."

A spokesman for the senator says Mr. Edelman's remarks are "at once both outrageous and dangerous." Those terms are entirely appropriate and may, in fact, understate the risk the Edelman letter poses to our way of life and all that our fighting men and women are risking, have risked, and have lost in Iraq.

After the South was defeated in our Civil War, the scapegoat was Confederate president Jefferson Davis, and the ideas of the "Lost Cause" and "Jim Crow" were born.

After the French were beaten by the Prussians in 1870 and 1871, it was the imaginary "Jewish influence" in the French army general staff, and there was born thirty years of self-destructive anti-Semitism, culminating in the horrific Dreyfus case.

After the Germans lost the First World War, it was the "back-stabbers and profiteers" at home on whose lives the National Socialists rose to prominence in the succeeding decades and whose accused membership eventually wound up in torture chambers and death camps.

And after the generation before ours, and leaders of both political parties, escalated and reescalated and carpet-bombed and re-carpet-bombed Vietnam, it was the protest movement and Jane Fonda and—as late as just three years ago—Senator John Kerry who were assigned the kind of blame with which no rational human being could concur, and yet which still, across vast sections of our political landscape, resonates unchallenged and accepted.

And now Mr. Bush, you have picked out your own Jefferson Davis, your own Dreyfus, your own "profiteer"—your own scapegoat.

Not for the sake of this country.

Not for the sake of Iraq.

Not even for the sake of your own political party.

But for the sake of your own personal place in history.

But in reaching for that place, you have guaranteed yourself tonight not honor, but infamy.

In fact, you have condemned yourself to a place among that remarkably small group of Americans whom Americans cannot forgive: those who have sold this country out and who have willingly declared their enmity to the people at whose pleasure they supposedly serve.

A scapegoat, sir, might be forgivable, if you hadn't just happened to choose a prospective presidential nominee of the opposition party.

And the accusation of spreading "enemy propaganda that the United States will abandon its allies in Iraq, much as we are perceived to have done in Vietnam, Lebanon and Somalia" might be some day atoned for, if we all didn't know—you included, and your generals and the Iraqis—that we are leaving Iraq, and sooner rather than later, and we are doing it even if to do so requires, first, that you must be impeached and removed as president of the United States, sooner rather than later.

You have set this government at war against its own people and then blamed those very people when they say "Enough."

And thus it crystallizes, Mr. Bush.

When Civil War general Ambrose Burnside ordered a disastrous attack on Fredericksburg in which twelve thousand of his men were killed, he had to be physically restrained from leading the next charge himself.

After the First Lord of the British Admiralty, Winston Churchill, authored and enabled the disastrous Gallipoli campaign that saw a quarter-million Allied soldiers cut down in the First World War, Churchill resigned his office and took a commission as a frontline officer in the trenches of France.

Those are your new role models, Mr. Bush.

Let your minions try to spread the blame to the real patriots here, who have sought only to undo the horrors you have wrought since 2002.

Let them try it until the end of time.

Though the words might be erased from a million books and a billion memories, though the world be covered knee-deep in your lies, the truth shall prevail.

This, sir, is your war.

Senator Clinton has reinforced enemy propaganda? Made it impossible for you to get your ego-driven, blood-steeped win in Iraq?

Then take it into your own hands, Mr. Bush.

Go to Baghdad now and fulfill, finally, your military service obligations.

Go there and fight your war. Yourself.

24

Bush Is Just Playing Us with "Troop Withdrawal"

September 4, 2007

You watch a stalker extract sensitive knowledge about his or her subject from sources who never even become aware they are sources, and you wonder why the stalker could not redirect these energies into useful—and presumably lucrative—endeavors.

You watch the B student who seems to do nothing but cut classes and cut corners, and you know in your heart that the slightest increased effort on the student's part would produce A's, and you wonder why that 1 percent growth in self-expectation cannot be summoned.

And you watch a Bush administration devoted not merely to misleading the public but, seemingly with almost religious fervor, to improving the science of misleading the public, and you wonder what good they might have actually done in the world if they had focused those not unimpressive skills on leadership or statesmanship rather than sleight of hand.

Such it was around Labor Day, as Robert Draper's book *Dead Certain* revealed the reality behind the administration's almost poetic manipulation of the country into believing there would be some kind of reevaluation of Iraq in September. Gradually the falsely inflated expectations had been reduced from the dangling carrot of a major withdrawal, to the promise of a "Petraeus report," to the somewhat less impressive truth that the report would not be written by General David Petraeus, to the stark, stinking bottom line: the "report" would be an opening statement and a lot of politicking by a serving officer whom the president should have kept out of politics at all cost.

And thus Draper's book—and the sinister image of President Bush "playing" to stay in Iraq so that his successor would be forced to stay in Iraq—and a quote not only never denied by the White House, but shortly thereafter repeated, almost word for word, by one of his advisers.

And thus another holiday milestone, and the regrettable need for yet another Special Comment.

AND SO HE IS BACK from his annual surprise gratuitous photo op in Iraq, and what a sorry spectacle it was. But it was nothing compared to the spectacle of one unfiltered, unguarded, horrifying quotation in the new biography to which Mr. Bush has consented.

As he deceived the troops at Al-Asad Air Base yesterday with the tantalizing prospect that some of them might not have to risk being killed and might get to go home, Mr. Bush probably did not know that, with his own words, he had already proved that he had been lying, is lying, and will be lying about Iraq.

He presumably did not know that there had already appeared those damning excerpts from Robert Draper's book *Dead Certain*.

"I'm playing for October–November," Mr. Bush said to Draper. That, evidently, is the time during which he thinks he can sell us the real plan, which is "to get us in a position where the presidential candidates will be comfortable about sustaining a presence."

Comfortable, that is, with saying about Iraq—again, quoting the president—"stay . . . longer."

And there it is. We've caught you. Your goal is not to bring some troops home, maybe, if we let you have your way now. Your goal is not to set the stage for eventual withdrawal. You are, to use your own disrespectful, tone-deaf word, playing at getting the next Republican nominee to agree to jump into this bottomless pit with you and take us with him, as we stay in Iraq for another year, and another, and another, and anon.

Everything you said about Iraq yesterday, and everything you will say, is a deception, for the purpose of this one cynical, unacceptable, brutal goal: perpetuating this war indefinitely.

War today, war tomorrow, war forever!

And you are playing at it! Playing!

A man with any self-respect, having inadvertently revealed such an evil secret, would have already resigned and fled the country! You have no remaining credibility about Iraq.

And yet, yesterday at Al-Asad, Mr. Bush kept playing, and this time, using the second of his two faces.

The president told reporters, "They [General Petraeus and Ambassador Ryan Crocker] tell me, if the kind of success we are now seeing continues, it will be possible to maintain the same level of security with fewer American forces."

And so Mr. Bush got his fraudulent headlines today: "Bush May Bring Some Troops Home."

While the reality is, we know from what he told Draper that the president's true hope is that they will not come home, but that they will stay there, because he is keeping them there now, in hope that those from his political party fighting to succeed him will prolong this unendurable disaster into the next decade.

But, to a country dying of thirst, the president seemed to vaguely promise a drink from a full canteen—a promise predicated on the assumption that he is not lying.

Yet you are lying, Mr. Bush. Again. But now we know why.

You gave away more of yourself than you knew in the Draper book. And you gave away more still on the arduous trip back out of Iraq— hours in the air—without so much as a single vacation.

"If you look at my comments over the past eight months," you told reporters, "it's gone from a security situation in the sense that we're either going to get out and there will be chaos, or more troops. Now, the situation has changed, where I'm able to speculate on the hypothetical."

Mr. Bush, the only "hypothetical" here is that you are not now holding our troops hostage. You have no intention of withdrawing them. But that doesn't mean you can't pretend you're thinking about it, does it?

That is your genius as you see it, anyway. You can deduce what we want. We, the people, remember us? And then use it against us.

You can hold that canteen up and promise it to the parched nation. And the untold number of Americans whose lives have not been directly blighted by Iraq or who do not realize that their safety has been reduced and not increased by Iraq, they will get the bullet points: "Bush is thinking about bringing some troops home. Bush even went to Iraq."

You can fool some of the people all of the time, can't you, Mr. Bush? You are playing us!

And as for the most immediate victims of the president's perfidy and shameless manipulation of those troops—yesterday sweating literally as he spoke at Al-Asad Air Base, tonight again sweating figuratively in the Valley of the Shadow of Death—the president saved, for them, the most egregious "playing" in the entire trip.

"I want to tell you this about the decision, about my decision about troop levels. Those decisions will be based on a calm assessment by our military commanders on the conditions on the ground, not a nervous reaction by Washington politicians to poll results in the media."

One must compliment Mr. Bush's writer. That, perhaps, was the mostly perfectly crafted phrase of his presidency. For depraved indifference to democracy, for the craven projection of political motives onto those trying to save lives and save a nation, for a dismissal of the value of the polls and the importance of the media, for a summary of all he does not hold dear about this nation or its people, nothing could top that.

As if you listened to all the "calm assessments" of our military commanders rather than firing the ones who dared say the emperor has no clothes, and the president no judgment.

As if your entire presidency was not a "nervous reaction," and you yourself nothing but a Washington politician.

As if "the media" does not largely divide into those parts your minions are playing, and those others who unthinkingly and uncritically serve as your echo chamber, at a time when the nation's future may depend on the airing of dissent.

And as if those polls were not so overwhelming, and not so clearly reflective of the nation's agony and the nation's insistence.

But this president has ceased to listen. This president has decided that night is day and death is life and enraging the world against us is safety. And this laziest of presidents actually interrupted his precious time off to fly to Iraq to play at a photo opportunity with soldiers, some of whom will on his orders be killed before the year—maybe the month—is out.

Just over five hundred days remain in this presidency. Consider the dead who have piled up on the battlefield in these last five hundred days.

Consider the singular fraudulence of this president's trip to Iraq yesterday, and the singular fraudulence of the selling of the Petraeus report in these last five hundred days.

Consider how this president has torn away at the fabric of this nation in a manner of which terrorists can only dream in these last five hundred days.

And consider again how this president has spoken to that biographer: that he is "playing for October–November." The goal in Iraq is "to get us in a position where the presidential candidates will be comfortable about sustaining a presence." Consider how this revelation contradicts every other rationale he has offered in these last five hundred days.

In the context of all that now, consider these next five hundred days.

Mr. Bush, our presence in Iraq must end. Even if it means your resignation. Even if it means your impeachment. Even if it means a different Republican to serve out your term. Even if it means a Democratic Congress and those true patriots among the Republicans standing up and denying you another penny for Iraq, other than for the safety and the safe conduct home of our troops.

This country cannot run the risk of what you can still do to this country in the next five hundred days.

Not while you are *playing*.

Conclusion

The Nexus of Politics and Terror

Relieved of orange, yellow, and red alerts, relieved of hovering attorneys general and shoot-from-the-hip vice presidents, the *ex*-secretary of Homeland Security could reflect, and reveal.

In retrospect, the quickly forgotten color-coded threat chart perplexed Tom Ridge. "More often than not," he said on May 10, 2005, "we [in the Department of Homeland Security] were the least inclined to raise it."

One pictures the jaw of the interviewer slowly dropping. "Sometimes we disagreed with the intelligence assessment. Sometimes we thought even if the intelligence was good, you don't necessarily put the country on [alert]." One imagines Ridge looking dreamily into the distance as the reporter goes ashen, then faints. "Some people were really aggressive about raising it [the threat level], and we said, 'for *that*?'"

You know what, Tom? *I* said that, too. And I'm still saying it. Thanks for backing me up there.

There *are* terrorist plots.

And there *are* successful terrorist plots.

And, perhaps worst of all, there are successful terrorist plots pulled off by idiots. It can be argued that for any cleverness they showed, all of the 9/11 bombers were idiots—if their understanding of the extremist interpretation of their religion was wrong just in the *slightest,* they not only murdered and terrorized, but they also killed themselves for *nothing.* No starker definition of idiocy is possible.

It is indeed possible that a moron throwing lighted matches toward a barrel of gasoline against a gale force wind might still actually succeed in blowing up the barrel. Even a jackass who puts cleaning powder in an envelope and mails it to a newscaster can claim to be a successful terrorist, as can the chowderheaded newspapermen who publicize the act.

Never should we let our guard down; never should we dismiss the improbable or fantasy-driven plots of terrorist wannabes—they might just be stupid enough to succeed.

But that doesn't mean that every time we learn of one of their daydreams, our government should publicize, even boast of, "interrupting a terrorist plot." As Roman emperor and unintentional philosopher Marcus Aurelius so incisively noted, we each encounter dishonesty, greed, selfishness, and falsehood every day. If we're still surprised that it happens, *we* are now supplying the surprise.

Thus the concept of our *Countdown* series "The Nexus of Politics and Terror." If a guy decides he wants to blow up the moon by shaking up a bottle of Coke with Mentos mixed into it, and the Department of Homeland Security arrests him and crows about stopping "a dangerous terrorist," *who* is supplying the terror? And to what end?

"The Nexus of Politics and Terror" has never been about dismissing terror plots. It's about dismissing a government that proudly exposes every ludicrous scheme as if it were Osama bin Laden's most labyrinthine plan. Any such government shows itself either incapable of discriminating between potentially deadly criminals and nuts with more pipe dreams than pipe bombs, or exploiting the concept of terror to make sure we stay scared, 100 percent of the time. In so doing it is asking us to surrender first our common sense, then our ability to discern, and finally our freedom.

"Better safe than sorry" ignores a disturbing truth about the days since September 11, 2001. "Safe" and "sorry" are not mutually exclusive nor mutually inclusive. We can be safe, and still very sorry indeed—and we can be sorry, and still anything from safe.

So, as I have presented them on *Countdown,* here are the fourteen prime examples into August 2007, when the juxtaposition of "terror plot" revelations and the political need for smokescreens and diversions were the most blatant. As I caution each time we air this compilation: There is every reasonable chance that the malefactors accused intended all manner of heinous results. There is also a reasonable chance that a similar chronological list could be constructed out of "terror plot" revelations and the openings of Dairy Queens around the country.

But most important, if only one of these examples is, in fact, the exception to the logical fallacy—if it's actually true in any instance that A happens, then B happens, and A really *did* cause B to happen—then we need to urgently question just what the Department of Homeland Security has been doing all this time, and whether or not it is really here to ameliorate fear or, in fact, to perpetuate and focus it.

These are not doubts that there are terrorists. These are a collective answer to Tom Ridge's somewhat dim-witted, whispered, rhetorical question: "For *that*?"

Number One, May 18–21, 2002: On May 18, the first details are disclosed of "The President's Daily Briefing" of August 6, 2001, including its ominous but evidently ignored title "Bin Laden Determined to Strike in U.S." The same day, another memo is discovered revealing that the FBI knew of men with links to al-Qaeda who were training at an Arizona flight school. The memo has never been acted upon. In short, questions about 9/11 intelligence failures are swirling.

Two days later, on May 20, FBI director Robert Mueller declares that another terrorist attack is "inevitable." The day after that, the Department of Homeland Security issues warnings of attacks against railroads nationwide, and against such New York City landmarks as the Brooklyn Bridge and the Statue of Liberty. On the twenty-third, another diaphanous warning is made: that there may be terrorist scuba divers in unnamed waters lurking like some jihadist Jaws. No attempt against railroads, infrastructure, or Robert Shaw's boat are mounted, and the only arrest that even seems to overlap any of the dire pronouncements is of an Ohio man vaguely connected to al-Qaeda who was trying to ascertain if he could pull his vehicle over to the side of the Brooklyn Bridge and, using blowtorches, destroy the giant bolts and cables that have kept the structure's tension braced against the bridge's suspension cables since 1883.

Number Two, June 6–10, 2002: Coleen Rowley, an FBI agent who had tried to alert her superiors to the specialized flight training taken by Zacarias Moussaoui, testifies before Congress on June 6. Senate Intelligence Committee chairman Bob Graham says Rowley's testimony, which suggests the government missed the chance to disrupt the 9/11 plot, has inspired similar whistle-blowers.

Four days later, on June 10, Attorney General John Ashcroft conducts a highly unusual news conference in Russia. "We have," he insists by satellite, "disrupted an unfolding terrorist plot." Ashcroft reveals that an American named Jose Padilla is under arrest, accused of plotting a radioactive "dirty bomb" attack in this country. In fact, Padilla has by now already been detained for more than one month; the Bush administration has suddenly and inexplicably decided to reveal this fact, at this particular point, *after* Rowley's testimony.

Number Three, February 5–10, 2003: On February 5, Secretary of State Colin Powell tells the United Nations Security Council of Iraq's concealment of weapons, including its eighteen "mobile biological weapons laboratories," justifying a U.N. or U.S. first strike. Many in the U.N. are doubtful. Months later, much of the information is proved untrue, and even Secretary Powell will later admit that this most public pretext for war was, at best, erroneous. After Secretary Powell's speech on the fifth, antiwar demonstrations around the globe crest.

Two days later, on February 7, Homeland Security secretary Ridge cites "credible threats" by al-Qaeda and raises the terror alert level to orange. "Take some time," Ridge says affably, "to prepare for an emergency." Three days after that, Fire Administration head David Paulison (who will become the acting head of FEMA after the Hurricane Katrina disaster) advises Americans to stock up on plastic sheeting and duct tape to protect themselves against radiological or biological attack.

One rural Connecticut homeowner promptly sheathes his house in plastic—on the *outside*—not realizing that the only value such "defense" could conceivably offer is if the plastic were posted on the *interiors* of windows and air vents.

Number Four, July 23–29, 2003: The White House admits on July 23 that the CIA, months prior to the president's State of the Union Address, expressed strong doubts about the claim that Iraq had attempted to buy uranium from Niger.

The next day, the preliminary version of the congressional report on the 9/11 attacks is issued. It criticizes government at all levels. It reveals that an FBI informant had once lived with two of the future hijackers, and concludes that Iraq had no link to al-Qaeda. Twenty-eight pages of the report are redacted.

On July 26, American troops are accused of beating Iraqi prisoners.

On July 29, after a week of headlines that have begun to shake the country's confidence in the Bush administration, *NBC Nightly News* begins with Tom Brokaw intoning: "Word of a possible new al-Qaeda attack." The Department of Homeland Security issues warnings of further terrorist attempts to use airplanes for suicide attacks.

Number Five, December 17–21, 2003: On December 17, 9/11 Commission co-chair Thomas Kean says the attacks were preventable. The next day, a federal appeals court says the government cannot detain suspected radiation bomber Jose Padilla indefinitely without charges, and the chief U.S. weapons inspector in Iraq, Dr. David Kay, who has previously announced he has found no weapons of mass destruction there, announces he will resign his post.

On December 21, the Sunday before Christmas, four days after yet another cluster of news headlines that have eaten into the administration's credibility, Homeland Security director Ridge again raises the threat level to orange, claiming credible intelligence of further plots to crash airliners into U.S. cities.

Subsequently, six international flights into the United States are canceled after several passenger names are purportedly found to have produced matches on secret government "no-fly lists." The French later identify those matched names: One belongs to an insurance salesman from Wales, another to an elderly Chinese woman, a third to a five-year-old boy.

Number Six, March 30–April 2, 2004: The new chief weapons inspector in Iraq, Charles Duelfer, tells Congress on March 30 that we have still not found any WMD in that country. And after weeks of refusing to appear before the 9/11 Commission, Condoleezza Rice relents and agrees to testify.

On March 31, four Blackwater USA contractors working in Iraq are murdered. Their mutilated bodies are dragged through the streets and left on public display in Fallujah. The role—and safety—of civilian contractors in Iraq is now widely questioned.

Two days later, on April 2, the FBI and Homeland Security issue bulletins warning that terrorists may try to blow up buses and trains using fertilizer-and-fuel bombs (like the one detonated in Oklahoma City) stuffed into satchels or duffel bags.

Number Seven, May 16–26, 2004: On May 16, Secretary of State Powell appears on *Meet the Press.* Moderator Tim Russert asks Powell about the personal credibility the secretary had risked while laying before the United Nations the supposed "case" against Saddam Hussein. An aide to Powell suddenly interrupts the question, claiming the interview has exceeded its predetermined length.

Russert: "I think that was one of your staff, Mr. Secretary. I don't think that's appropriate."

Powell: "Emily, get out of the way."

Secretary Powell finishes his answer, making the stark admission that much of the information he had been given about weapons of mass destruction in Iraq was "inaccurate and wrong and, in some cases, deliberately misleading."

Five days later, new photos showing mistreatment of Iraqi prisoners at Abu Ghraib prison are released. Then, on May 24, Associated Press video from Iraq confirms that U.S. forces mistakenly bombed a wedding party, killing more than forty.

Two days after that, Attorney General Ashcroft and FBI director Mueller hold a joint news conference to warn, in Ashcroft's phrasing, that intelligence from multiple sources "indicates al-Qaeda's specific intention to hit the United States hard," and that 90 percent of the arrangements for an attack on this country were complete.

Despite this extraordinary statement, the color-coded terror-threat status is not raised, and the secretary of Homeland Security, Tom Ridge, does not even attend the announcement.

Number Eight, July 6–12, 2004: On July 6, Democratic presidential candidate John Kerry selects Senator John Edwards as his vice-presidential running mate, producing a small bump in the election opinion polls and a huge swing in media attention toward the Democratic campaign to unseat President Bush.

Two days later, on July 8, Ridge is back before the microphones.

"Credible reporting," he asserts, "now indicates al-Qaeda is moving forward with its plan to carry out a large-scale attack in the United States." He adds that attacks are anticipated in the summer or autumn.

Four days after that, the head of an obscure new agency, the U.S. Election Assistance Commission, Deforest B. Soaries, Jr., confirms he has written to Ridge about the prospect of postponing the upcoming presidential election in the event it is interrupted by terrorist attacks.

Number Nine, July 29–August 1, 2004: At their party convention in Boston on July 29, the Democrats formally nominate John Kerry as their candidate for president. As in the wake of any convention, the Democrats dominate media attention during the subsequent weekend.

But on Monday morning, August 1, just three days later, Homeland Security raises the alert status for financial centers in New York, New Jersey, and Washington, D.C., to orange. Secretary Ridge boldly announces that new information has come from "as reliable a source— a group of sources—as we've ever seen before."

Reliable or fictitious, the evidence supporting the warning— reconnaissance data left in a home in Iraq—later proves to be roughly four years old and largely out of date.

Number Ten, October 6–10, 2005: At 10 A.M. EDT on October 6, President Bush addresses the National Endowment for Democracy, once again emphasizing the importance of the war on terror and claiming his government has broken up at least ten terrorist plots since 9/11.

At 3 P.M. the same day, just five hours after the president's speech began, the Associated Press reports that Karl Rove will testify again before the grand jury investigating the leak of the identity of covert CIA operative Valerie Plame Wilson, and that special prosecutor Patrick Fitzgerald has told Rove he cannot guarantee that he will not be indicted.

At 5:17 P.M. EDT the same day, just slightly more than seven hours after the president's speech began, New York officials disclose a bomb threat to the city's subway system, based on information supplied by the federal government. Within minutes—even as New York police officers deploy to subway stations to begin random, high-profile searches of bags and parcels—a spokesman for the Department of Homeland Security says the intelligence upon which the disclosure is based is of doubtful credibility.

And later it emerges that New York City had known of the threat for at least three days and had increased police presence in the subways long before making the announcement at that particular time. Local New York television station WNBC reports it had the story of the threats *days* in advance of the announcement, but was asked by high-ranking federal officials in New York and Washington to hold off on the story. Additionally, at least two "insiders" had been informed of the subway rumor as early as October 3 by family or other connections to Homeland Security. The information recipients had in turn sent e-mails to friends and relatives no later than October 5, tipping them off at least a day before the general public had been given any clue. There was now a structure in place in which, at least in theory, whether or not you were a friend or relative of somebody at Homeland Security might determine whether you would live or die.

Less than four days after having revealed the threat, New York mayor Michael Bloomberg says, "Since the period of the supposed threat now seems to be passing, I think over the immediate future we'll slowly be winding down the enhanced security." Meanwhile news organizations, ranging in credibility from the *New York Post* to NBC News, quote sources who say there was reason to believe the informant who triggered the warning had simply made it up. A senior U.S. counterterrorism official tells *The New York Times*, "There was no there there."

Number Eleven, August 9–14, 2006: The controversy over warrantless domestic surveillance is cresting when, on August 9, the day after the Connecticut Democratic senatorial primary, Vice President Cheney says the victory of challenger Ned Lamont over incumbent Joe Lieberman is a positive for the "al-Qaeda types," who, he says, are "clearly betting on the proposition that ultimately they break the will of the American people, in terms of our ability to stay in the fight."

The next day, August 10, British authorities arrest twenty-four suspects in an alleged imminent plot to blow up U.S.-bound aircraft using liquid explosives smuggled on board in sports drink bottles. Domestic air travel is thrown into chaos as carry-on liquids are suddenly banned.

On August 14, British intelligence reveals it did not think the plot was imminent—only the U.S. did—and that American authorities pressed to make the arrests immediately. Eleven of the twenty-four suspects are later released, and in the months to come, the carry-on liquids ban is incrementally relaxed.

Number Twelve, May 7–9, 2007: On May 7, after Greensburg, Kansas, has been leveled by a tornado, the state's governor notes, more in sorrow than in anger, that the redeployment of so much of the Kansas National Guard and its matériel to Iraq might now cripple the soldiers' ability to respond were another disaster to hit her state. "What we're really missing is the equipment," says Democrat Kathleen Sebelius. "And that is putting a strain on recoveries like this one."

The next day, the authorities announce arrests in a far-fetched plan to attack soldiers at Fort Dix in New Jersey. The so-called terrorists planned to gain access to the base by posing as pizza deliverymen—but their plan, incredibly, was *not* a suicide mission. They state clearly that they intended to kill personnel and then retreat to safety, even though they were going to attack a closed compound full of trained soldiers with weapons.

And though counterterror authorities brand the scheme "sophisticated," its perpetrators were not sophisticated enough to have considered it might be counterproductive to hand over a videotape of themselves training with weapons to a Circuit City store in order to be transferred to DVD. A store clerk is called "alert" for noting that the men have handed him a tape full of homemade videos of *themselves* wearing military outfits and head coverings and shooting off automatic rifles.

The saga of "The Fort Dix Six" and the Circuit City hero not only erases from most news coverage the issue of disaster readiness in Kansas, but it also obscures a story the next day: that in anticipation of his testimony to a House panel about the political purges of United States attorneys around the nation, Attorney General Alberto Gonzales has submitted opening remarks that match, virtually word for word, the remarks he gave the previous month to a Senate committee. The Fort Dix story is still lingering on May 9, when Gonzales actually testifies.

Number Thirteen, June 2–3, 2007: On June 2, another far-fetched plan is revealed: a scheme to blow up the jet fuel pipeline feeding John F. Kennedy International Airport in New York City, thus causing the entire airport to be consumed in a horrific conflagration that was intended to also destroy part of the borough of Queens. One of the men arrested is a past airport employee who once had access to the sprawling complex, but his knowledge of the pipeline system appears to have been limited to having looked at it from a distance.

The manager of that system tells *The New York Times* that the pipeline is not some kind of fuse. Shutoff valves throughout its length would have easily contained any damage, just as a leak in a tunnel in any city would not flood everything in that city belowground.

The dramatic if somewhat impractical plot again anticipates—and obscures—the next day's headlines. June 3 is the day of the second Democratic Party presidential debate. And at a time when the scandal over the firings of U.S. attorneys and their replacements by political operatives is continuing to unfold, the "JFK Plot" happens to be publicly announced by the Bush-appointed U.S. attorney for Brooklyn, New York.

Standing by his side to authenticate the seriousness of the physically impossible plot is the police chief of New York City, who by sheer coincidence is the father of a correspondent for Fox News Channel.

Number Fourteen, July 22–25, 2007: The new biography of Vice President Dick Cheney is the lead story on the talk shows and newscasts of Sunday, July 22, and the following day. Even a sympathetic author such as Stephen Hayes concludes that George W. Bush may be, at best, a co-executive with Vice President Cheney.

The next day, Attorney General Gonzales testifies before the Senate Judiciary Committee in such a convoluted and contradictory fashion that even Republican senator Arlen Specter tells him that his "credibility has been breached to the point of being actionable." Gonzales has previously testified that he did not know of any major dispute within the Justice Department over the domestic spying program. But the former deputy attorney general, James Comey, contradicted him with the story of a 2004 dispute so overwhelming that several Department of Justice officials threatened to resign. But now Gonzales insists again to the Senate that the dispute was *not* about what Gonzales pedantically insisted was the official "Terrorist Surveillance Program" (as opposed to the generic "terrorist surveillance program"), and that Comey is in error. Gonzales is warned by Democrats that he may have made himself liable to a perjury charge.

And also on July 24, President Bush tries to conflate al-Qaeda and al-Qaeda In Iraq: "Those who justify withdrawing our troops from Iraq by denying the threat of al-Qaeda in Iraq and its ties to Osama bin Laden ignore the clear consequences of such a retreat. If we were to follow the advice, it would be dangerous for the world—and disastrous for America."

Bush's issue, not Gonzales's, controls the news media. In addition to the president's speech, the 24th sees a Transportation Security Administration bulletin warning of what appeared to be terrorist "pre-attack security probes and dry runs" that has been leaked to a succession of journalists, beginning with several at NBC News.

Even though the bulletin is four days old and the *ninety-first* such memo issued by the TSA in the first seven months of 2007, it is reported, repeatedly and breathlessly, for the next several days. It describes "recent suspicious incidents at U.S. airports" and "the unusual nature and increase" in items intercepted by airport security that resemble bomb components.

Most notable of the items recovered from passengers' luggage in four incidents: wires embedded in cheese, and items containing clay. The theory is that each is the shape and consistency of bomb components, and terrorists might be testing to see whether they could successfully pass them through screening devices, or to determine screeners' and counterterror officials' reactions to their discovery.

Though one waggish federal official downplays the bulletin to NBC News by joking, "I fear no cheese," the story of dry runs is broadcast and printed with full credulity. By the end of the week, however, it turns out that one of the most suspicious items—"clay" encased in a small plastic pouch—is, in fact, a cold pack whose contents have leaked and dried on the outside of the pouch. Its possible dry-running passenger proves to be a grandmother from Long Island who says she was interrogated at the San Diego airport after her leaky pain reliever was discovered. The first question she was asked: "Do you know Osama bin Laden?"

And thus is it never a crime to question, never a crime to doubt, never a crime to keep grains of salt at the ready.

It was, after all, this nation's *first* secretary of Homeland Security who asked the most important and the most rational of all questions:

"For *that*?"

Acknowledgments

If you'll do me the favor of reading them, these might constitute the oddest collection of acknowledgments you'll ever see.

In addition to the collected thank-yous, a few acknowledgments of fact are merited:

—that there are terrorists;

—that there is a need to revise some of our expectations of our rights in the wake of how our century has thus unfolded;

—that this all would have been taken a lot more seriously if the Bush administration had deemed "homeland security" a nonpartisan issue, and had a few members of the other party help lead the defense (you know, the way most presidents have done during—and I use this term because the administration has been so fond of it—wartime);

—and, most important, that just because the previous three things are true, that no more means we now have to surrender the Constitution or the two-party system than did the reality of the Cold War or the presence of the anarchists of the late nineteenth century or the existence of the "Secesh" movement.

We should also acknowledge, of course, that even the most enlightened government of all time was, by definition, a collective defense against fear of some kind. The best of them are in the protection game. The worst supply both cause and effect.

Now my expressions of gratitude. For pure patriotic inspiration: John Dean, Joe and Valerie Wilson, Elizabeth Edwards, and the high school teachers who opened my eyes to the incredible usefulness of history, particularly Walter Schneller and Peter Gibbon.

Among the staff of *Countdown:* our executive producer, Izzy Povich, and Greg Kordick, Denis Horgan, Rich Stockwell, Tina Cone, Eelin Reily, Brendan O'Melia, Jonathan Larsen, Carey Fox, Brian Nalesnik, Joelle Myszka, David Shuster, and Monica Novotny. Among our analysts: Craig Crawford, Roger Cressey, Lawrence O'Donnell, and Richard Wolffe. Among our MSNBC and NBC management: Jeff Zucker, Phil Griffin, Steve Capus, Bill Wolff, Cheryl Gould, Dan Abrams, and Neal Shapiro. And on the mother ship: Brian Williams, Andrea Mitchell, and Mike Boettcher.

Externally: my agent, Jean Sage, and my literary agent, Esther Newberg; the editor who coaxed a book out of all this, Tim Bartlett; and my friends Richard Lewis, Jeff Wald, Dan Patrick, Jason Bateman, Aaron Sorkin, and the late Hal Fishman. From the political arena: the Clinton family (especially Dorothy Rodham), Al Gore, John Kerry, Joe Biden, Harry Reid, and Dennis Kucinich.

Thanks also to all the visitors to YouTube, Crooks and Liars, Daily Kos, and every other website and viewer and reader who passed along links and videos. And of course, a man I never met but who I hope would approve: Edward R. Murrow.

And last and foremost, Katy Tur, who managed the seemingly mutually exclusive roles of girlfriend and editor ("I love it. Too long"). My eternal thanks, Bear.

ABOUT THE AUTHOR

KEITH OLBERMANN is the host of *Countdown with Keith Olbermann* on MSNBC. A veteran broadcaster, he was the co-anchor (with Dan Patrick) of ESPN's *SportsCenter* from 1992 to 1997 and helped to launch ESPN2 and ESPN Radio Network. Olbermann is the recipient of numerous awards in radio and television broadcasting, including the Edward R. Murrow Award for his coverage of the events of 9/11. He has hosted prime-time news programs, moderated a debate between Democratic presidential candidates, anchored the World Series broadcast, and written for dozens of publications, including *The New York Times*, *Newsweek*, *Time*, and *Sports Illustrated*. He co-hosts MSNBC's election night coverage and NBC's *Football Night America*.

ABOUT THE TYPE

The principal text of this book was set in Fairfield, the first typeface from the hand of the distinguished American artist and engraver Rudolph Ruzicka (1883–1978). Ruzicka was born in Bohemia and came to America in 1894. He set up his own shop, devoted to wood engraving and printing, in New York in 1913 after a varied career working as a wood engraver, in photo-engraving and banknote printing plants, and as an art director and freelance artist. He designed and illustrated many books, and was the creator of a considerable list of individual prints—wood engravings, line engravings on copper, and aquatints.